Page 147

THE FOUR WHEEL DRIVE STORY

THE
FOUR
WHEEL
DRIVE

A CHAPTER IN
COOPERATIVE ENTERPRISE

STORY

by HOWARD WILLIAM TROYER

McGraw-Hill Book Company, Inc.

NEW YORK   TORONTO   LONDON

1954

THE FOUR WHEEL DRIVE STORY
A Chapter in Cooperative Enterprise

Library of Congress Catalog Card Number: 54-7361

to Walter A. Olen

PREFACE

This is the story of a small business that became big. It is not unique, for in its essential pattern the same story has occurred during the past fifty years in dozens or even hundreds of towns and villages throughout the country.

It is the story of a man and his family, but, more than that, it is also the story of a community, and of a dozen neighbors—a machinist, a young attorney, the village druggist, the proprietor of a lumberyard, the newspaper editor, and others—who, uniting their energies and savings, built a multimillion-dollar industry producing a product serviceable to mankind from Narvik to Patagonia. No single one of them could have done it alone. Nor was the task that they together accomplished assured of easy success. But out of joint endeavor—through trial and error, through failure and triumph, through the vision and courage of men working together—came modern America: the urban community with its schools and hospitals, its hard-surfaced and well-lighted streets, the well-turned and well-graded highways linking community to community, the parkways and sunlit residential areas—all of them a symbol, less of free than of cooperative enterprise.

It is a story typical of second-generation Americans, the children of immigrants from Norway and Sweden, from Germany and England, mingling, working together, finding themselves, and from hardships and privations of a remembered frontier extracting the courage and determination to build a world fulfilling their forefathers' dreams—that life for their children and their children's children might be more bountiful than it had been for them.

It is in one sense, too, a very simple story. There are no mysteries and few miracles, and the dissidence, when it occurred, grew out of misunderstanding rather than malice. It constitutes in itself a record of a changing era. It is—to use a phrase too often misappropriated and misconstrued—a story of the American way of life.

Any book, and particularly one like this, is written by many people: by all the men and women who lived the events its pages recount, by those who kept a careful daily record, by those who remember, and by all those who care that the story of our past, the way of a free society, be preserved. I am grateful to Walter A. Olen, always interested and helpful, who with an inherent sense of honesty and fair play has from the beginning insisted upon the objectivity of the record; to his sons, Robert A. Olen and Donald B. Olen, for their interest; to Clarence Zachow and P. J. F. Batenburg, for much material on the early years; to Floyd Hurley, James Sorenson, Joseph Leyrer, Arthur E. Johnson, Edward Wandtke, Arthur Danley, and dozens of others, employees in the company and citizens of Clintonville, whose names are not mentioned either here or in the Notes and

Acknowledgments but whose friendly assistance and help has been indispensable; to Mrs. Edythe Vaughan, secretary to Mr. Olen, and to Chester Cook of the Pacific Four Wheel Drive Auto Company of San Francisco and Los Angeles; to William J. Cronin, James F. Wheeler, and Christy Borth of the Automobile Manufacturers' Association; to Melvin E. Bartz, Francis M. Higgins, Donald B. Olen, and Horace Vaile for reading the manuscript in its entirety; and to D. G. T., whose patient assistance, as always, has been invaluable.

HOWARD WILLIAM TROYER

CONTENTS

THE FOUR WHEEL DRIVE STORY

Clintonville, Wisconsin, Circa 1905

In the year 1905 the little town of Clintonville, lost in the blueberry bogs and sandy hills of central Wisconsin, numbered 480 families, or, as Frank Gause, the country clerk, had it, 1,837 souls. Its unpaved main street was a clay mire in late winter and early spring, dry and dusty as a country road in summer and fall. From the banks of the Pigeon River, where the early lumbering village had sprung up, the street angled three-quarters of a mile south to the higher ground which the Lake Shore and Western Railroad had in the seventies claimed for its right of way. Clapboard dwellings, straight-front shops, and a few two-story brick structures housing a department store and the offices of local doctors and lawyers still clustered near the river, though ever since the railroad had come, it had been slowly pulling the town away from its earlier lumbering site.

There were the usual shopkeepers. The largest place in town, a department store, was run by C. F. Folkman. John Kalmes was the village druggist. August Gill and Sons sold

dry goods. H. W. Bohn ran the hardware. D. J. Rohrer
owned the sawmill and lumberyard. More integral to the
functioning village and the surrounding farms than in later
years were William Hoffman, the harness maker, and William Loaks, builder of wagons and buggies, whose large and
busy shop was near Hoffman's. Down a side lane near the
river stood the blacksmith and machine shop of Otto Zachow
and William Besserdich. Across the lane and halfway back
to Main Street was the office of the Clintonville *Tribune*, the
weekly newspaper, owned and edited by Joe Cotton.

Three years earlier, Joe Cotton, a tall, slender English-
man, had reversed the usual trend of the immigrant, and
with his young wife had left Labula, Iowa, where he had
taken his first job as printer's devil in the office of the Labula
Gazette at the age of eleven, and moved to Clintonville, buying himself half interest in the *Tribune*. Under his editor-
ship the paper had grown. Every Monday morning he set
out up Main Street, gathering the local news and soliciting
his advertisers. From Folkman's department store to George
Elermann's saloon, to the young attorneys, Olen and Olen,
for court news, and then on to Schauders' shoe store for
more advertising. The era of singing commercials had not
yet come to plague America, but the rhyming squib was
already potent, as indicated by the quatrain written by
young Cotton for the Schauders. What it also indicates is
the bilingual quality of the early community and the pre-
ponderance of German inhabitants.

> *Wir allen wüssen zwar auf Erden*
> *Wie diese Schub zu Staube werden—*
> *Doch Mensch! Willst du recht Lange laufen*
> *Müsst du von Schauder dir schube kaufen.*

In between canvassing the shopkeepers, Cotton recorded the news, stories of inclement weather and unusual rainfall, the deaths and marriages occurring in the village, fisticuffs in the local saloons or ballrooms, summertime dances and picnics, the Fourth-of-July celebration, for which in 1905 the oration of the day had been delivered by the young attorney Walter A. Olen.

Drunkenness and fights occurred frequently and made good copy. The issue of July 28 was enlivened by the story of how Fred Remling, "a dead-game boozer from Marion, was slid jailward by Justice James McNeil." When the Justice found young Remling slumped down to the boardwalk, hugging a telephone pole and refusing to move, he simply backed himself between the young man's legs and, using them as thills, pulled him along "on the west side of his trousers" until he was ready to get up and walk.

Several nights later there was a brawl at George Elermann's saloon, when Charles Ohms, stumbling along the bar already half drunk, reached into a glass bowl that contained tickets for a ball to be held upstairs later on that night. Ohms subsequently testified that he had merely happened to bump the bowl in lighting his cigar. George Elermann, the barkeeper, however, had reached across the bar and grabbed his arm, whereupon Alfonse Karczewski, standing alongside, had pitched in, grabbed the tickets away, and "meaning to be kind and considerate," assisted Ohms outside. It was, so Alfonse claimed later, Ohms's own drunken stumbling and falling against Mr. Guensler's barber pole that had broken two of his ribs. When Ohms charged Karczewski with assault and battery, the firm of Olen and Olen accepted and won the case for the defendant.

More numerous than the fights were the accidents caused by the running away of teams and horses. Late in July, Mrs. Hoeffs and Mrs. Krause, returning from the Ringling Brothers Circus, had their team frightened by a fluttering banner. Both women were killed and the vehicle demolished. The very next day a fractious pony driven by Mrs. Meiklejohn, in rounding the corner of Mill and South Pearl Streets, had run down Mrs. Delano, a pedestrian, causing a broken arm and cuts and bruises, and had thrown Mrs. Meiklejohn from the carriage, bruising her face and knocking out her teeth. The small son of Fred Retzner that summer lost both his legs in the sickle bar of a mowing machine when his father's team became frightened at a whip the young lad was carrying. And a following issue records the story of how a horse driven by Mrs. Knapp ran away and, dashing around a corner, threw Mrs. Knapp over the side of the carriage, so that her right ear, caught between wheel and buggy, was sheared off.

Reading the accounts, in which there is no suggestion that these events were considered to be extraordinary, one is less surprised by the sanguine suggestion of Thomas Edison, who even earlier had predicted that with the coming of the horseless carriage "the danger to life and limb will be much reduced."

As for horseless carriages (already known as automobiles), there were in 1905 fewer than three thousand of them in the state of Wisconsin, which already had a population of more than three million. There were none at all in the village of Clintonville. Later on that fall, though, the two young machinists of the Clintonville Machine Shop, Otto Zachow and his brother-in-law, William Besserdich, were thinking of enlarging their own trade, chiefly concerned with the repair of sawmills and threshing machines, to include the sale and servicing of automobiles. After considerable study and attendance at one or two auto shows in the East, they announced to their fellow villagers that they had taken the agency for the Reo, and by February of 1906 their neighbor and city editor, Joe Cotton, reported the imminent arrival of Clintonville's first car, "a handsome Reo, four seat runabout," selected largely because the car had just won the New York Motor Club's great six-day national economy tour by carrying four passengers 628 miles at a cost of $3.38 per passenger.

A week or so later, amidst considerable fanfare and with ample tooting of the bulbous horn strapped to the side of the driver's seat, Otto and William drove slowly up and down Main Street to the delight and admiration of their neighbors. Their first sale later on that spring was to W. H. Finney, one of the village doctors and already a man of many enterprises, including ownership of the Grand Theatre and the Ideal Bowling Alleys. The new car, fully described by Joe Cotton, was a maroon, four-seater runabout, weighing 975 pounds and powered with an 8-horsepower gasoline engine, capable of a speed of 26 miles per hour. Before the summer was out, three more cars had been sold and the villagers could begin to assess the likely permanence and value of the new arrivals for village life.

But not all was well. One of the first results had come when a horse driven by Henry Stock had taken fright at the new Zachow and Besserdich Reo parked in front of the latter's residence. Dashing through between auto and boardwalk, the horse had hit a telephone pole, come to an abrupt stop, thrown Mr. Stock over the dashboard onto his shoulders, broken from the thills, and left town with his tail high. A later accident involved Dr. Finney. Approaching a horse-drawn dray on a country road, Dr. Finney veered his car sharply to the side and had already passed the team when a third horse, being led along behind, took fright and leaped directly into the path of the car. The resulting impact frightened the team, and the whole rig dashed madly on down the hill, upsetting the wagon. The driver remained unhurt, though one of the horses was killed and the owner sued for $2,000. Dr. Finney promptly replied by asking for $500 for damages to his car. Quite coincidentally (and yet perhaps not quite, since similar incidents were occurring throughout the state), less than a month later the governor signed a new bill which made it mandatory for the motorist approaching a horse-drawn vehicle to stop his car, shut off his engine, alight, and assist the driver in leading his team past the automobile, on pain of being fined $25 to $100 or spending sixty days in jail.

Less hazardous to man and beast but equally discomfiting were the difficulties of the road, the sand hills and clay bottom lands lying beyond the village. Paved roads or even graveled ones were unheard of. In the summertime a 20-mile trip was a day's journey, and after a sudden rain, or in the spring and fall with the clay roads churned into a mire by hoof and wagon wheel, the new automobile was bound to get stuck. On a trip to Waupaca that first summer Dr. Finney and Walter A. Olen traveled as far as Manawa, a distance of 13 miles, before, as Mr. Cotton had it, "the car baulked at carrying both a doctor and a lawyer," and as they went up a long hill, sand got into the chain drive and ground the cogs off the sprocket wheel. The car had to be left waiting for repairs, and the men hired a farmer to drive them back in a buggy. On a second occasion Dr. Finney and Otto Zachow, returning from a trip to Marion, hit a late-spring thaw, the car sinking to the axles near the Tanner farm in Larabee. Late at night and with the nearby farmers sound asleep beyond the sound of the little bulb horn, both men worked all night, prying up the car with fence rails and limbs from nearby trees, before finally abandoning it and trudging on home in the breaking dawn.

Whether it was experiences such as these which first gave Zachow and Besserdich the idea for building a more power-ful car than the Reo they were selling is not definitely known. It seems likely enough; but it is one thing to know the limi-tations of a machine and still quite another to think through, to shape, and to design a better one.

For that process, however, both Otto Zachow and William Besserdich were particularly well-fitted and trained by their earlier experience. Otto had been born on a farm, where the skillful use of a pocketknife, a hammer, and a monkey wrench is learned almost in the cradle. At sixteen he had left his father's farm at Leppla's Corners and gone to Apple-ton, where he had been apprenticed to James Pardee, a blacksmith, for his board and room and a wage of $25 a year. After a year or two with Pardee he had moved on to work in a carriage shop, later on to the machine shops of the Union Pulp Company of Kaukauna and to the Valley Iron Works of Appleton, where he had helped to install the first hydroelectric-light plant in the country, before opening up his own blacksmith shop and wagon works in Bessemer, Michigan, with his brother-in-law, William Besserdich. William's own training had been somewhat similar. In 1891 they had moved their machine shop to Clintonville. For twenty years both men had been shapers and builders at the forge.

But neither one had yet hit on the idea that the superior car which they might build would be one in which the power would be applied equally to all four wheels. At what moment and to whom the idea first occurred is a matter of debate, and the story has been variously told. It was, however, in no sense a new matter. German engineers had been experimenting with such a design for some years, and many Americans, quite unknown to either Otto or William, or to each other, were busy, each with designs of his own. Otto Zachow's own story before he died—and no one who knew him ever doubted Otto's word—was that the idea had come to him on a trip to the city of Appleton. Appleton was then (as it is now) a city of ravines, and the relatives whom Otto and his wife drove down to see lived on the edge of one. Otto himself, after the usual ride around town for each one of the relatives, became interested, or rather lost, in the dexterity with which he could handle the Reo, and somewhat carelessly drove over the rim, the car sliding down the hillside into the ravine.

Seeing the even ground down below at the bottom of the ravine, Otto decided to drive on down and turn around and have the car climb back up the hillside. When he tried it, though, the front wheels, instead of lifting themselves upward, buried themselves in the hillside; and the back wheels became powerless. Studying the situation for a minute or two, he rejected the usual proffers of shovels and props, backed down again, turned the car around, and, with the power wheels lifting the weight upward rather than pushing it into the hillside, backed the car all the way to the top. It was on the way home that the full idea came to him. "Who is it," he said to William, "who ever heard of a mule walkin' on only two legs?"

Characteristically, he set to work at once on the problem of how to communicate power to the front, as well as to the rear, wheels. The difficulty, of course, would be in the steering, in keeping the front wheels capable of being turned while power was applied to a shaft like the one in the rear axle. For a week or two Otto kept working away—and then suddenly the problem solved itself. Taking an idea from the tumbling rods on an old-fashioned threshing-machine separator, Otto evolved a double-Y universal joint operating at the jointure of front wheel and axle, the joint itself, incased in a drop-forged ball and socket, permitting the wheels to turn without interfering with the transmission of power. Carefully and slowly he worked out his first design, then forged the ball and socket out of brass. The invention completed, there were two further steps to take. The device needed testing, and he himself needed a patent to protect his invention.

Of necessity the second took precedence over the first. The entire automobile industry at the moment was in a state of flux. A new idea might make a man a million dollars or, more likely, leave him bankrupt. New firms and manufacturers were sprouting everywhere, flourishing for a day but already spent and obsolete on the morrow. Such ideas as balloon tires and four-wheel brakes had already been discarded, though their revival a generation later brought millions to the reinventors. What a man needed who had faith in his idea was to protect himself until it was ready for the market.

Otto was a blacksmith and a machinist, not yet a manufacturer and certainly not a lawyer. He had told no one of his invention, but obviously sooner or later, if he was to market it, he would have to share it with the world. Thinking of the men in his own community, he turned to the young attorney Walter A. Olen. How does one go about patenting an invention, he wanted to know. Side by side, the two men sat for a long time by lamplight in Olen's upstairs office, facing the little round potbellied stove, and discussed the matter.

First of all, what they needed was a careful drawing and a detailed and accurate description. Then, since Olen and Olen were not patent attorneys, Walter would find a Washington patent firm to check on the matter. Then, if no one else had thought of the idea first, Otto would be free to go ahead and market his idea or manufacture his own automobile. The cost of the patent would not be prohibitive, but the chance for the successful manufacturing of an automobile in Clintonville was a matter Olen had never before contemplated and on which he could give no reassurance.

On the next morning, Otto, carrying his ball-and-socket invention in an old valise, boarded the Northwestern train for the city of Fond du Lac, where his son, an apprenticed machinist, was at work in the Northwestern Railroad shops, to secure the son's help in making the drawings. A week later he was back with his drawings, and the long process of securing the patents began.

Had Otto known the number of patents pending or already granted to men concerned with the principle of applying power to all four wheels of a vehicle, he might have been discouraged from the outset. Fortunately the revelation came slowly and over a period of time. Dozens of men, both American and European, had been working on the idea. As early as 1901 the first patents had been filed by Gustave Hoffman, a German citizen residing in England, and every year since had seen an increasing number of applications. Unfortunately, or perhaps fortunately for Otto, not one of them had been successful, and though all of them were concerned with the principle of providing "means for driving each of the four ground-wheels with equal power" and so preventing "the slipping of drive wheels on muddy or sandy roads or in hill climbing or skidding and sideslip when running an incline or in making abrupt turns," not one of them had come upon, or even near to, so simple and effective a design as his own.

But there were long delays and numerous letters to be received and written and applications to be filled and always the interminable waiting. And in the meantime there was sawmill and threshing-machine work to be done in the shop. The agency had been enlarged to include not only the Reo but also the Ford, and the new automobiles they sold had to be kept in repair. The record does not indicate how many new automobiles were sold, though probably not many, since Otto's time and attention seem to have been increasingly taken by the new car he was already designing in his mind and the drawings and parts he kept working away on in his spare time. William, however, kept up the agency, and in the summer of 1907 he drove Dr. Finney, whose Reo was now two years old, to Chicago, where they traded the car for a new White Steamer, "one of the finest cars that ever turned a wheel," according to the columns of the *Tribune,* "a perfect model of beauty and endurance."

When the patents finally came through in the summer of 1908—they had been filed August 1, 1907—Otto and William set to work on the new car in earnest, and gradually as the hammering and shaping and the grinding of the power-driven lathe continued, the news of what was going on down in the little machine shop began to spread uptown, at least as far as the office of the *Tribune.* By the middle of the winter the new chassis, complete with its four-wheel drive and a center transform case for the differentiating of power to the front and rear axles, necessary in negotiating turns and on uneven ground, was ready for assembly. Probably because of the interest in Dr. Finney's new Steamer, the new car was equipped with a steam-power plant, cross-compound in type, and the kerosene fires were ready to be lit under the boilers. Finally Saturday arrived. The fires were lit. The water began to turn into steam. Onto the dry-goods box fastened across the chassis in lieu of a seat climbed the two inventors. Slowly Otto adjusted the valves and shifted the levers. Joe Cotton, one of the few townspeople who had been let in on the secret, standing alongside, could hardly suppress his excitement. The car moved forward. The new four-wheel-drive principle was ready for its first practical test.

It stood it well. By the middle of the next week Joe Cotton was ready to tell the whole town of Clintonville. "They have plowed through snow drifts three feet deep," he wrote, "pushed huge billows ahead of them, gone over the roughest and most slippery roads and climbed the steepest hills at a twenty-five mile an hour clip. . . . There is talk of organizing a company. The car should be a winner from the word go."

The hopes were perhaps too sanguine. To be sure, the principle of applying power to all four wheels was easily demonstrable. The car could go where neither Ford nor Reo, nor Dr. Finney's White Steamer, nor Alex Stewart's new Rambler could follow, but the cross-compound steam engine was heavy and cumbersome and quickly out of repair. And if they shifted the power plant to a gasoline motor and paid the attorney's fees—$3 to Olen and $17 to the Washington patent lawyers—where would the time and money come from to build a second and a third car? For more than a year they had been puttering away to the neglect of their own business; and now, with a huge backlog of their own custom work still undone and their funds expended and many a bill still unpaid, how could they go ahead? It was a difficult question.

For a month or two Otto and William turned back to their custom work in a kind of feverish desperation, but when (though it was still unpaid for) the new body they had ordered for the chassis arrived in May, their hopes rose again. Joe Cotton described the new arrival in glowing colors:

> It surely is a dandy, deep maroon in color, large and roomy, holding eight people all told—two in front, four in the rear and two extra on folding seats. If the recently patented drive lives up to expectations, it will revolutionize the automobile business and place the inventors, Zachow and Besserdich, on easy street.

1 3

Always the talk of the easy millions lying ahead, but the immediate concerns to the inventors were time, materials, and money.

To allay some of the pressing demands, Otto and William turned again to the man who had bought their first Reo. With Dr. Finney they organized the Badger Four Wheel Drive Auto Company, with a capitalization of $35,000, Finney to put up a third of the cash as needed and Otto and William to surrender their patents and to provide the direction and labor, the custom work to continue, though the major object now would be the manufacturing of cars.

Nor did that solve all the problems. Always there were the feverish haste and anxiety lest, now that the patents were abroad, other companies ready with labor and capital might step in to exploit them. There were delays in securing material. There were still funds to be raised to pay off back debts, and though both men mortgaged their homes, even that did not suffice. There was the custom work to be done, with the customers angry and irritated at the delay. There was the man on the street who could not understand why, now that the company was launched, cars were not built overnight and sold to the waiting customers. Older makes of cars were sold daily and soon the market would be glutted. By the end of the year Dr. Finney, having already advanced a capital of some five thousand dollars without seeing any tangible results, became discouraged. There were misunderstandings and angry words among the partners. It was one thing, indeed, to conceive a new idea and even to build a working model of a machine and quite another to begin manufacture. Perhaps after all Zachow and Besserdich were no more than machinists and W. H. Finney but a doctor.

Had the whole company given up and dissolved and lost faith in the idea, it would have been no more than had already happened in dozens of towns to hundreds of ideas and new inventions. That in Clintonville it did not happen then—or some time later—owes itself to two factors: the faith of Otto Zachow and William Besserdich in their invention and the energy and organizing endeavor of a newcomer to the company, the young attorney Walter A. Olen.

Men Working Together

There is a rather widespread idea in America that an invention belongs, or ought to belong, solely to the inventor, though the records of our economic and industrial development deny it. What one man frequently cannot, many men working together often can do. We are fond of the adage of the mousetrap, but the fact remains that the path through the wilderness is more readily beaten if it happens to be a well-graveled or hard-surfaced road. In our own economic history more often than not it has been the energy and organization, the persistence and imagination with which markets have been sought out and created—as well as supplied—that have made an invention functional and profitable. In other words there is in nearly every company a role for the organizer or the promoter, and in the present instance it is difficult to believe that the principle and practice of applying power to all four wheels of a vehicle—the basic invention of the jeep—would have been available to America without the organizing genius, the enterprise, and the endeavor of Walter A. Olen.

Mr. Olen was reared in Wisconsin on a farm, where, he still likes to say jocularly, "all good people are born." His father, a young Norwegian ship's carpenter, had arrived in America in time to help fight the Civil War and when it was over returned to the shipbuilding yards on the Wolf River at Winneconne. There, like a good many other first-generation Americans, he had married one of his own group, a young Norwegian girl, Amelia Miller, and when the shipbuilding slackened off, turned to farming, buying himself a heavily wooded 80 acres on the shore of the lake. Walter was the first boy born on the farm though he already had two older brothers, Clarence and Otto.

It was a life of privation and hardship, not unredeemed, to be sure, by the boyhood pleasures of hunting and fishing, and the amenities of the family and neighborhood, games, berrypickings, and church sociables. As a young boy Walter drove the ox team yoked to his father's home-built trundle wagon as the whole family turned to, grubbing out the stumps and roots, to bring the land under cultivation. When the chinch bugs ate the wheat or the high water drowned out the corn, the family subsisted for entire winters on gruel and an occasional strip of salt pork or a rabbit brought in by the boys from hunting. When money became too scarce, the older boys worked for their neighbors as hired men and the father took a job as a millwright in Winneconne, leaving the chores and the farm work, the harvesting of the grain and the cutting and husking of corn, to Walter and his sister, Nora.

It is not surprising, as our own grandfathers have frequently admonished us, that children reared in such circumstances develop enterprise. Walter's first job, with the work done for the week and Saturday morning's kindling split and piled, was to go around among the neighbors selling Perfection Dyes. On a lucky afternoon he would make as much as 30 cents, which he shared with his younger sisters if they had helped him in piling the wood. Later on he added writing paper, pencils, and ink to his line and raised the average profits to a dollar, and still later, permitted by his father to put out a setline, he caught quantities of catfish and sturgeon, which he dressed and peddled in the neighborhood, lugging them around on a home-built wagon in a large milk can filled with water.

In the wintertime the children walked 2 miles to a log schoolhouse, though later on a new building was erected within three-quarters of a mile of the farm. It was there, at the Ball Prairie School, that Walter achieved his first distinction by winning a community spelling bee open to adults as well as to children, entitling him to represent the district at a county-wide contest in Oshkosh. It was there, too, that he got his taste and enthusiasm for reading. From his older brother, Otto, himself an excellent student, later a teacher and an organizer of community debates, he acquired a love of oratory and a respect for exact information. Having graduated from the Ball Prairie School, Walter moved to Winneconne to attend high school; he earned his room and board by doing chores and minding store and paid for his books and clothes by walking out of town in the evening to husk corn by moonlight. The furniture store and undertaking establishment was owned by an uncle, and Walter worked at making picture frames, recaning chairs, filing saws, and assisting in laying out the dead. The cot he slept on stood in the back room of the store among the empty coffins.

Before he had finished the two years at Winneconne, Walter passed the examination for a teacher's license, left school, and began teaching. His first job was in the Tuller District, near Neenah, for $25 a month, $10 of which went for board and room. He upped that the next year to $40 a month when he trudged to a log schoolhouse halfway up the state, hired for his "physical fitness to give" the seventy-two pupils "the discipline they needed." With what he saved from his winter's teaching, he attended Oshkosh Normal in the summer. He also began reading law on the side, and three years later enrolled in the Northern Indiana Law School at Valparaiso, Indiana.

He graduated with the highest distinction awarded at the time, that of being selected by the senior class and the faculty for the honor of being speaker at the annual Memorial Day exercises, held jointly by the university and city, an event memorable enough to have the chief justice of the supreme court of the state as the main speaker. Having worked at a dozen different odd jobs to support himself, including running a boardinghouse and clerking in a department store, Walter now traded all the clothes he already had for a new suit, a black swallowtail, suitable for the occasion. On the eventful day he spoke to seven thousand people, was carried back to the university on the shoulders of his comrades, and a week later, wearing the new suit on his back as his only luggage, began the long, dusty walk back home to Wisconsin.

Because he had no money to open a law office, he went back to teaching school for a year, and then, having passed his examinations and being admitted to the bar, he decided to settle in Clintonville. The decision was made on his way home from a teaching job at Seneca. While riding in a caboose from Marion to Clintonville, he had become acquainted with a Catholic priest, Father Bastian, who told him they needed a new and honest lawyer in the town, one of the present ones having been disbarred for embezzlement and a second suspended. His brother Otto, too, earlier that year had opened an office at Manawa, and they agreed that after deciding which of the places seemed the more likely, the two of them would get together and establish a firm.

On the first day in Clintonville Walter spent $30 of the $40 he had saved to begin practice—$6 for two weeks' room and board, $3.50 for office rent for a month, $5 for an ad in the Clintonville *Tribune*, $7 for *Wisconsin Statutes*, $6 for Bryant's *Justice*, $1 for a code practice, $1.50 for letter-heads and a sign to go over the door. In the first three months of practice he lost his first case but averaged about $16 a month, mostly on collections and real-estate commissions. By the end of the first year, he had a fair business. At the end of the second, Otto moved over from Manawa and the sign over the door read "Olen and Olen." In the next five years the firm prospered, and by 1905 the two brothers had become the leading attorneys of the town.

One of the conclusions Walter Olen had come to as a young man was that he would not get married until he possessed $5,000 either in cash or in property with which to support a wife and family. By 1908 he felt that at least in part he had accomplished what he had set out to do, and some time before the patents for Zachow and Besserdich had been granted, he and his bride, Cora Miller, a Clintonville girl whom he had married a few weeks earlier, left for a trip to the West Coast. He was gone a full year, working

20

part of the time for a law firm in Portland and later on investigating and staking out two timber claims, one for his wife and one for himself, in Klickitat County, Washington.

It was shortly after his return that Otto Zachow came to see him once more, and again the two men sat side by side around the little potbellied stove in the upstairs office. Otto Zachow was discouraged. He told Walter the story of how he and William and Dr. Finney had organized the Badger Four Wheel Drive Auto Company. But the second car was still not completed and already the company was falling apart. Dr. Finney had become impatient and refused to advance any more money. The debts were mounting. Otto had long since mortgaged his house for its full value and William had done likewise. The custom work at the machine shop had fallen off, and what there was they had no time to do if they were to continue to work on the car. Dr. Finney had gone so far as to retain an attorney to protect his rights during the dissolution of the company. He, too, wanted a lawyer.

The men talked until well after midnight. Walter had a real admiration for Otto, who was the older, a soft-spoken, mild-mannered German, slow and deliberate in his actions but an excellent mechanic and a man whom he had always known as thoroughly honest.

"Do you still believe that your principle is sound?" he asked him.

"That I do," said Otto.

"And that you can work out a practical and expedient way to build automobiles?"

"If I have time," said Otto.

"Does Finney believe in the invention?"

"I'm afraid not, not any more," said Otto. "He thinks he's going to lose—"

"That's the real trouble," said Walter. "You don't need one man who believes in you, you need a dozen. What you need is capital and workmen. Let me think it over."

The next morning Walter went to call on Dr. Finney to hear his side of the story. All he wanted was to get out, he said; all he'd ask for was his money back. Then Walter continued to make the rounds. He went to see Joe Cotton at the *Tribune*. He called on the lumber-mill owner, D. J. Rohrer. The next day he dropped in to see Charley Folkman, the owner of the department store, and the druggist, John Kalmes, and then way up at the other end of Main Street, Frank Gause, the stationmaster for the Northwestern. For a week or two the talking continued. Did any of them believe sufficiently in the patents of Zachow and Besserdich and in the car already built to help underwrite the venture? Should they all go together and organize a new company? Back in 1904 William Lewis had borrowed $75,000 to start building Mitchells and in three years was building 300 cars a year and in five, the capital of the company had risen to $1,000,000. Over at Hartford (Wisconsin) the Kissel Company had been organized four years earlier, built two cars in the first year, seventeen in the second, and 120 in the fourth, and had been offered a $250,000 bonus to move to Dubuque. Should they along with Otto and William constitute the nucleus of a group to reorganize the company, take it to the Clintonville Advancement Association, and put on a city-wide drive to raise funds?

Walter could be persuasive. He was a gifted speaker, and his energy and optimism pervaded the group. Zachow and

Besserdich were at once more hopeful and enthusiastic. Walter's legal mind was busy working out the details. This time they would need plenty of working capital, perhaps 1,000 or 1,100 shares at $100 a share. They would have to reimburse Dr. Finney for all he had spent before they could dissolve the old company. Otto and William could retain 350 shares for their patent rights, the machine shop, and the car they had already built. The rest of them could perhaps subscribe for 50 shares and raise $5,000, part of it to be paid out of a commission they would receive for selling the remainder of the stock to the public. Perhaps the Clintonville Advancement Association could be interested in providing them with a site for the factory.

At a meeting of the Association in April of 1910 the plans for the reorganization of the company were announced. Seven men had, or were willing to subscribe for, 43 shares, or $4,300, providing others in the city would come in for an equal amount. Stock to the value of $35,000 was to be set aside for the owners of the patents and the builders of the car. Five of them would undertake to sell $35,000 worth outside of the city.

"In this I feel we are all working together," said Walter, who was the speaker for the occasion.

> None of us is wealthy and we do not want any wealthy men in our company. . . . I have faith in Otto Zachow and William Besserdich and in the car they have built. When you are called upon to help, don't get out an axe or a sledge hammer. Don't break down; build up. We can build a factory here and make one of the finest automobiles on the earth. It will employ many men. It will make money for you. It will bring many changes to the city and make Clintonville known throughout the world.

In order to be sure that the city would not lose its enthusiasm, Walter wrote dozens of letters to nearby cities, describing the invention and the plans for the reorganization of the company and the building of a factory. In the next weeks delegations arrived from Oshkosh, Fond du Lac, Appleton, Plymouth, Port Washington, and a dozen other towns and cities within a radius of a hundred miles, eager to look over the plans, to have a look at the machine shop, to see the first car pull its way through sand and mud, and to stop and talk about the inducements their own cities might offer to have the company move bag and baggage to a new location. Spurred by the fear of losing the company, the Clintonville Advancement Association hurriedly assembled a committee to study sites and to secure options on land that might be suitable for the building and tendered to the company.

Walter also wrote hundreds of letters to prospective stock buyers in the state and throughout the country, though the first actual stock sold to anyone outside the city went to an uncle of Joe Cotton, A. J. Copp, then visiting his nephew. A week or so later Henry Hartel of Stevens Point drove down and electrified the little group by subscribing for 10 shares and paying half of it down in hard cash. Then Charles Hagen, a box manufacturer of Black Creek, became interested and agreed to take 20 shares, 25 per cent down. By the middle of June the reorganization of the company and the raising of the initial capital seemed assured. This year's Fourth-of-July celebration would be bigger than ever.

In order to arrange for it properly, the date was moved to the fourteenth and designated as "Big Booster Day" to celebrate not only independence but the organization of the new company. Seven thousand people attended the festivities, which officially began at three o'clock in the morning with the lighting of the fires for the roasting of the beeves in the barbecue pits. At nine in the morning a parade of floats, decorated by the business firms and led by the bands of Clintonville and Embarrass, and followed by the new Four Wheel Drive car and then dozens of others, wound its way down Main Street. At noon under a big circus tent in the square in front of the high school four thousand people were served free barbecued beef sandwiches with rye bread and pickles from the H. J. Johannes Pickling Works. Promptly at twelve the motorcar tests were held down at the sand pit at the west end of Menasha Street, where car after car—Imperials, Hudsons, Halloways, Fords, Buicks, Cadillacs, and a two-cylinder Brush—drove into the bottomless sand, stalled, tried to back up, tried to move forward, heated its motor, ground its wheels, and finally gave up to be pulled out by the new Four Wheel Drive auto to the cheers of the crowd, "mad with enthusiasm."

At two the first meeting of the stockholders in the new company was held in the Grand Theatre under the sponsorship of the Advancement Association. The old officers and directors resigned. Otto Zachow and William Besserdich officially surrendered and assigned to the new company their patent rights. Julius Prenzlow was unanimously elected to the chair and declared all offices vacant. Then nominations and balloting began. Seven new directors were elected, Walter A. Olen, D. J. Rohrer, H. B. Anabel, John Kalmes, Frank Gause, Charles Topp, and Charles Hagen. The capital stock was fixed at 1,100 shares at $100 a share, or $110,000.

Following the meeting came the horse races and wrestling matches, water fights between firemen, wire walking across the Pigeon River, a baseball game between the Browns and Blues, and later on in the evening free fireworks and two grand balls, one at Thurk's Hall and the other at the Opera House. "Clintonville has thrown off its shackles, that have fettered it in the past," Joe Cotton wrote the next morning for that week's issue of the *Tribune,* "has drunk at the fountain of youth, and started out with the banner of progress flying to make a city of itself."

When the new board of directors met, they elected Walter Olen president of the company, John Kalmes vice-president, Frank Gause secretary, and D. J. Rohrer treasurer, and moved to proceed in the manufacture of seven passenger cars, roadsters, runabouts, limousines, and landaulets, to sell for $4,500 with full equipment. In August the board moved to secure a site for the building of a factory, and a special meeting of the stockholders in September officially changed the name of the company to the "Four Wheel Drive Auto Company." In November H. B. Anabel was elected general manager and was asked to give his full time to the company—the only one of the directors who did so; the board moved to consider a site of 8½ acres to be paid for by public subscription; and by March of 1911 they were ready to let the contract for a factory building to cost $8,790.

The struggle to get the company onto its feet, however, was by no means over. It had been relatively easy to get the earlier subscribers to sign up for stock, but to get them to pay for the stock they had subscribed for was another matter. Many a man signed up for 10 shares but paid in less than $50. He had expected to get rich quickly and to let the earnings of the company pay for the rest of the stock, and he would wait now to see how the whole thing turned out, he said. The building of the cars was delayed by the necessity of selling more stock. H. B. Anabel, with William Besserdich as driver, toured the countryside with the first car, giving rides and demonstrations, to sell stock. "Your machine came down here with streamers flying in the wind," an angry Appleton man whose horses had been frightened wrote back. Otto with two mechanics tried to run the factory. W. A. Olen, still practicing law, gave up his own work to join Anabel in selling stock.

Sure of its own patents and seeking to spur interest in its product, the company offered to pay $1,000 to any automobile able to follow the Four Wheel Drive car for 10 minutes. But the takers of the challenge, hundreds of them, consumed time. Joe Cotton kept recording the episodes in the *Tribune*. One day it would be a Stanley Steamer and the next day a Buick, and the day after that it might be a Mitchell or a Reo. To outrun its challengers, the original Four Wheel Drive car ran through impossible sand pits, into mudholes of mire and clay, up the steepest hills surrounding every city within 200 miles of Clintonville. In the summer of 1911 it stalled 116 rear-driven cars trying to follow it, though it was never itself stopped in 12,000 miles of such tests. But wear and tear on the car necessitated repairs, and they, too, helped to run up the expense.

There were internal quarrels among the stockholders. Some of them, of course, had paid in more cash than the others and jealously guarded their own interests. When a minority group learned that the arrangement with the original promoters had been a commission of 10 per cent to be paid for in stock, they were outraged and called for a special meeting. One of the directors asked to resign and to have his stock canceled. He was refused. There was much trading and selling of stock among local stockholders and the price rapidly declined. One of the directors moved that all stock subscribed and not paid for be canceled or that the manager take whatever legal steps were necessary to force payment on delinquent subscriptions. Then the company began borrowing money for current expenses, covering it with mortgages on the factory and on the unfinished cars.

"I have not been in Clintonville for three months," wrote one of the out-of-town stockholders, to Walter A. Olen,

> and I have not herd anything about the Four Wheel
> Drive only some knocking on it. You are a lawyer and
> I would like a little of your advice. I got a letter from
> the company and Anabels' name as Gen. Manager and
> as there is some money dew from me he wrote for it but
> I am tempted not to put any more money in it as I say
> I have herd nothing but knocking on it since I am up here.

The attitude was typical.

The first car built for sale to the public was finally finished late in the summer and sold to August Matuzczak of Clintonville for a small down payment, the rest covered by a mortgage. The second car was not completed until late in the winter, nor sold until well into the next year. Indeed, it is almost incredible—what with the delays in manufacturing and the difficulties in selling stock or collecting money for that already sold; with mounting debts and mortgages and a steady decline in the price of the stock; with the stockholders discouraged and disgruntled—that the company survived the first year. It took courage to keep on going, and a kind of bullheaded tenacity.

In the middle of the summer, when H. B. Anabel, the

general manager, had resigned, the company had faced a crucial decision. Walter A. Olen had been president from the time of reorganization, but he himself was an attorney with a business of his own. The law had been and still was his first interest. The first inclination of any man—seeing how things were going—would have been to remain in his own profession. After all, he was simply an investor like the others. On the other hand he had been responsible for the initial move in organizing the new company. He had persuaded his neighbors to invest their savings. He was, as president, responsible, he felt, to the stockholders and to the town. Moreover, he still had faith in Otto Zachow and the invention. In July he surrendered his law practice and dissolved the firm, agreeing to give his full time to the Four Wheel Drive Auto Company, assuming the duties of the general manager, as well as the presidency of the board.

As general manager he made two astute moves. Sensing the growing interest in trucks and trucking vehicles—an industry lagging some ten years behind the development of pleasure cars—he persuaded the stockholders, in what seemed to many of them throwing good money after bad, to change their original directive, calling for seven cars, to include a 2-ton truck, and, as general manager, promised Otto Zachow a $450 bonus if the truck could be completed by the next February. The second thing he did was to hire, impulsively, P. J. F. Batenburg, a foreigner, almost at first sight.

Peter Johannes Frederick Batenburg had been born in Holland, son of a well-known surgeon with a family of nine children. Forced to shift for themselves, the boys had spread out over Europe, Peter himself, interested in and studying the growing automobile industry, going to Germany, Italy, and then to France. In Paris, quite by chance he had met a Catholic priest from Kimberly, Wisconsin (who later persuaded two of Peter's brothers to emigrate to America), and, talking to him about the automobile industry, the priest had told him about a new factory he had heard they were building up at Clintonville. Two months later Peter Batenburg had landed in New York and moved on to Detroit, surviving on ham and eggs—the only item he could make out on an English menu—and discouraged there because of his inability to speak English, had come on to Kimberly. A stranger in a new country and moneyless, he finally secured a job in an Appleton garage, sleeping in the upstairs room of a young baker who let him have the bed at night, since the baker himself slept during the day. After a month or so at the garage, he had secured the position of chauffeur with the Baldwin family of Appleton, driving their brand new Pierce-Arrow.

It was on one of the frequent Four Wheel Drive test climbs later on that summer that Peter Batenburg first met Walter A. Olen. The challenger that day was an Imperial touring car and the test run was up a long sandy hill. There were the usual onlookers, Peter among them. The Imperial had stalled on the first try, but a heavy intermittent shower had drenched the Four Wheel Drive and William Besserdich in attempting to start it had flooded the engine. Peter Batenburg had stepped in, introduced himself, suggested that all the spark plugs be wiped dry, adjusted the carburetor, and the car not only climbed the hill, but later successfully pulled the Imperial to the top. Discovering that Peter Batenburg was not only a chauffeur but also an engineer with European experience, Walter A. Olen hired him on the spot, and shortly after that Mr. Batenburg became the factory superintendent.

Peter Batenburg was a prodigious worker, an exacting taskmaster, sometimes tyrannical with the men under him, but he could relieve the general manager from the details of manufacturing for the work of promotion and advertising and the selling of stock, and for the first time the work in the shop began to hum. In August of 1912 Walter A. Olen, Peter Batenburg, and William Besserdich drove the first Four Wheel Drive car to the state fair at Milwaukee for the auto show, where the "weather god ruled in its favor." Among the forty automobiles on the test run in the 3-inch mud of the race track, the Four Wheel Drive was the only one that could prevent itself from slewing and skidding; it finally reached a speed of 48 miles per hour, while high above the crowd Lincoln Beachy in his biplane "swooped down like a hawk and then rose high in the air, as both of them circled the track." It was an auspicious occasion, and the men from the company gave out 9,500 booklets and 1,200 large catalogues describing the "most successful and most beautiful car at the fair."

It was not, however, in the pleasure cars, in the "roadsters, runabouts, limousines and landaulets," that the future of the new company lay. It lay in the odds of Walter A. Olen's gamble (odds attested to by the later interest of the U.S. Army) that the four-wheel-drive principle might be more suitable for a truck.

By late fall of 1911 there were nearly 700,000 licensed motorcars in the United States. Of the two million miles of public
roads, however, less than 10 per cent had been improved and
almost none hard-surfaced; and of the remainder more than
half, or well over a million miles, were still, as an irate
motorist insisted, "practically impassable seven months out
of the year." As for the motor-truck industry, it had lagged
sadly behind. The total number of trucks in operation during the year was roughly 25,000, though a good share of
them were no more than pleasure cars reconverted by sub-
stituting an open platform or a truncated wagon box for the
rear seat on a touring-car chassis.

Of the 25,000 trucks the United States Army owned
twelve. Three of them had been purchased by the Quartermaster Corps for use (within depot areas) at San Francisco,
one for Fort Sam Houston in Texas, and one for the Military
Academy at West Point, and seven for use at Manila. The
standard equipment for all overland or field transportation

at the time was still the four-mule escort wagon and the six-mule army wagon, and as late as the summer of 1911 specifications for a standard mule-drawn vehicle had been compiled and three of the leading manufacturers were building wagons to be tested in September on a long march with troops starting from Fort Riley, Kansas.

Within the Quartermaster Corps at Washington, D.C., however, things were already astir. There, Captain A. E. Williams, a motor-minded, lanky, six-foot-two West Pointer from North Carolina, on loan to the Quartermaster Corps from the 19th Infantry, had been busy preparing specifications for a type of motor truck that might eventually—at least so he dared hope—replace the mule-drawn wagon for the use of an army in the field. Largely through his own interest and insistence, and owing somewhat to his own persuasive powers with his superiors, the Quartermaster Corps was in the process that summer of purchasing two trucks for experimental and testing purposes, and Captain Williams, who had already written an article for the *Infantry Journal* on the possibilities of motor transportation replacing the army mule, was busy laying plans for a motor-driven vehicle test run of his own.

To secure more vehicles for the run, he had persuaded the Quartermaster Corps to invite the leading automobile manufacturers of the country to enter their own cars, and to further the project he himself had taken to the road, visiting the factories and talking over Army requirements with the manufacturers. In spite of his own enthusiasm, however, the project had moved slowly. Many an automobile manufacturer grew wary as he became more fully acquainted with what Captain Williams proposed to do. They were confident of the performance of their cars on a hard-surfaced road, where the going was easy and the footing sure, but to take off in the middle of winter on an overland run over unimproved roads, through ice and snow and spring rains, wasn't even good horse sense. They listened politely, seemed interested, but in the end declined the gamble.

It was on the way back to Washington from Milwaukee that Captain Williams, somewhat discouraged and debating the abandonment of his own idea, first read the advertisement of the Four Wheel Drive Auto Company. What interested Captain Williams immediately was the company's insistence that its product had the ability to climb through sand and snow or mud and rain—an insistence capped with what must have seemed at the moment a rather fantastic challenge, that it could go wherever any team of horses was ready to lead the way. The Captain was ready to be convinced, and he had no sooner returned to Washington to confer with his superior, Gen. James B. Aleshire, Quartermaster General, than he set out again for Wisconsin.

In Clintonville he was dumbfounded. To be sure, the new 44-by-66 factory building was nearing completion—the factory whistle having blown for the first time on December 20. But beyond that the only visible assets of the company were the old Zachow and Besserdich Machine Shop, two pleasure cars already built and one sold, and five others in various stages of manufacture. The surprise came later on that morning when Frank Dorn, a slender, cocky lad of twenty-four, now the company driver, proceeded to load down one of the newly built touring cars with eight men and drove the Captain out over the wintry roads to McNutt Hill, the heavy car frequently breaking through the surface crust into the mud below. In the afternoon, the car now loaded down with 1½ tons of scrap iron, Dorn and the Captain turned off the main road, driving through unfrozen sand pits, across plowed fields and mudholes, and finally back in town, up the concrete steps of the Lutheran church with the rear wheels resting on glare ice, until, as Captain Williams reported to his chief, "the whole thing bordered on the miraculous."

Unlike many of the other manufacturers of motorcars, Walter A. Olen and the other directors were ready to welcome a U.S. Army test, and excited enough by the Captain's visit and the Army's interest to present him with the car on the spot, had it not been for pending mortgages. Captain Williams himself hurried back to Washington, once more filled with dreams of his own test run, and within two weeks, a record time for having persuaded his superiors, the order for a stripped-down chassis and spare parts came through.

The car was shipped to Washington on January 14, 1912, P. J. F. Batenburg leaving a few days later for the capital to supervise the unloading and a few preliminary tests. A few days later he wrote from Washington to Walter A. Olen and the other directors, characterizing his experience in his own inimitable way:

> This morning we loaded the car—a little over 2,000 pounds —went with car and every hill was taken, then over very loose clay. When we went to a place where last year a river was. We sink't in over the differentials. I had no chains on and a wonder the car pulled out! Bravo! But then I sink't in again and was stuck, so I thought. All four wheels spinning. I could not touch ground. . . . What I did now? Put chains on my wheels (only on the front)

and my steel horse came alone out of his bad place. You understand our success!

Excitement ran high in Clintonville. When the test run was finally approved by the War Department and ordered by the Chief of Staff on February 6, Walter A. Olen himself left for Washington to be present for the starting ceremonies.

In the convoy, as it was finally assembled, were four trucks: a 1½-ton White; a 1¼-ton chain-drive Sampson; the reconverted Four Wheel Drive touring car; and a 1½-ton Autocar. A fifth, an assembled truck by the Wilcox Truck Company, had been abandoned the day before. Among the drivers, in addition to Captain Williams, were James Gaughan on the Four Wheel Drive; A. J. White on the Sampson; George Breitweiner and Michael Keating on the White; and S. N. Pringle and Joe Brown, company representatives for the Autocar, the only truck entered under private auspices.

Partly as a result of Captain Williams's own enthusiasm, and partly no doubt out of a sincere effort on the part of superiors to curb it, the test run set up and approved by the Army authorities was a severe one. For the cars and trucks, reconverted to carry a standard army wagon box and loaded with supplies and a ton and a half of sand ballast, the proposed route cut through the state of Virginia into North Carolina and then southwesterly across the mountains to Atlanta, and so northward again, through Tennessee and Kentucky to Fort Benjamin Harrison, near Indianapolis, a run of nearly 1,600 miles, over almost wholly unimproved roads, in the middle of winter with spring rains and thaws waiting for them on the northward leg of the journey.

"Now, then, Captain," General Aleshire is reported to have admonished Williams, "just as soon as your trucks get stuck down there in the mud, you wire me, and I'll send the mules to pull you out."

On the first afternoon the convoy made 33 miles to Dumfries, Virginia, without incident save for shearing off the bolts on the driving shaft of the Autocar. On the second day, 2 miles out of Dumfries, on a road that hadn't been improved since it had been traveled by the armies of Lee and Grant, as Captain Williams reported to his superiors, the Sampson, swerving sharply, cut out over an ice-covered ditch, crashing through into the 4 feet of water and mud below. After an hour's work with the block and tackle, the car was finally righted and the convoy proceeded, crossing the 4-foot ford on Chopawamsic Creek, and then pulling up a long, steep, ice-covered hill that proved the final undoing of the Sampson—the long, steady grind burning out the connecting-rod bearings. Abandoning the car, the party went on to Stafford Courthouse, where they halted for the night, the second day's drive having taken them exactly 16 miles.

On the third day Captain Williams, sending the Four Wheel Drive and the Autocar on to Fredericksburg, a distance of 10 miles, returned with one of the drivers in the White truck to the abandoned Sampson, and towing it to the nearest railway station, made arrangements for shipping it back to Washington, later on in the afternoon rejoining the others at Fredericksburg. On the fourth day, Sunday, February 11, the convoy rested. On the fifth the remaining three trucks reached Richmond, a distance of 60 miles, the going having been over fairly good roads save for a rough stretch of 15 to 20 miles.

On the sixth day, rolling along over the improved road from Richmond, Virginia, to Roanoke Rapids, North Carolina, the convoy made its best run on the entire trip, a distance of 98 miles without mishap, testimony to the excellent state of the highway being the three pleasure cars the convoy met en route, the only cars encountered throughout the entire run except those on the macadamized streets of the bigger cities.

It was down below Roanoke Rapids, on the country roads leading through Vaughn and Henderson and Wake Forest to Raleigh, North Carolina (a total distance of 78 miles), that the trucks encountered the first real hazards. On February 15 the caravan left Vaughn in a light rain which increased steadily and froze as it fell, until telegraph poles and trees along the road began to go down under the heavy burden. The truck wheels became solid cakes of ice and the roads so heavy that it was necessary to run in low gear continuously. On the next day near Franklinton, where the roads had recently been worked and graded, the red mud lay axle-deep, and the only forward movements possible necessitated hitting the mud under full power, plowing ahead a few feet, backing up, and shoveling out the mud before plunging forward again; and when on one occasion a 6- to 8-foot fill proved completely impassable, the alternative lay in taking a wide circuit through the woods, crossing a stream on an improvised bridge, and so back to the highway again before going forward. Whenever one of the other trucks floundered hopelessly in the tractionless mud, the Four Wheel Drive with the block and tackle and a nearby telegraph pole for anchor did double duty in righting it, until in one particularly tough stretch it twisted off its own transmission shaft and had to be towed into Wake Forest, where it was left waiting for parts to be sent out from the factory.

The White and the Autocar arrived at Raleigh on the seventeenth. By the nineteenth the Four Wheel Drive had been repaired and rejoined the others. On the twentieth the convoy left Raleigh for the 300-mile run across the mountains to Atlanta, Georgia. Twenty-five miles out, again in a pouring rain, the roads became so heavy the trucks had to proceed in low gear even going downhill. The only difference between the road and the open fields, as one of the men said later, was that the road had signposts on it and the fields had not. Farmers along the route shook their heads sadly at the fools from Washington, one of them remarking, as he came up to the stalled trucks, that he would not attempt hauling an empty wagon over roads like that, not even with his mules.

On succeeding days the steady grind in axle-deep mud, plus the double-duty towing, led to breakdown after breakdown. The Four Wheel Drive, ascending Morgan Hill on the morning of February 23, once more twisted off its driving shaft and was left waiting for repair parts near Greensboro. Before the parts arrived, the White truck—the entire convoy having made less than a hundred miles in five days— broke down and was towed into a farmyard. As a matter of fact, it seems somewhat doubtful that the test run might ever have been completed if it had not been for Walter A. Olen and the directors of the Four Wheel Drive Auto Company, who finally, upon their own repeated and insistent request, were permitted to send out Frank Dorn, the young

driver whom Captain Williams had met earlier at Clintonville, to join the company.

Dorn arrived at Greensboro on the twenty-fifth. What he
found, as he wrote to his sister, was

> a bunch of inexperienced government greenhorns trying
> to drive three trucks through acres of bottomless red clay.
> They have had three weeks of solid rain here and the
> cars sink out of sight in the mud. The local farmers put
> five bags of wheat on a wagon and hitch four mules on
> to pull it through. No wonder the trucks have been having
> trouble.

Part of the trouble, though, as Dorn came to see at a
glance, lay in the driving. As he said later on,

> What them government boys did was every time they
> come to a mudhole and the radiator began to sink out of
> sight, was to goose up the gas lever and send her roarin'
> in, in high, till she stopped. Then they'd roar her back
> in reverse, skid the wheels and have her dig in, or if they
> got back a foot or so, roar her up again and hit the mud
> like a stone wall.

Frank had been driving for the company for over a year
and had picked up a trick or two. Moreover, he had been
sent out by the company on a special commission—$75 a
month and expenses for the trip, and another $75 a
month if he brought the Four Wheel Drive through on her
own power. "Move over!" he said to Jimmie Gaughan, who
had been driving the car, and then proceeded to show the
other drivers how to do it. The secret was not to race the
engine and not to hit the mudhole in high. A long steady
slow pull with all four wheels at work could take the Four
Wheel Drive through any mudhole on the road, that he

knew, and the Four Wheel Drive being through, the others could follow, and if they couldn't, they could be towed.

That Dorn himself knew what he was up to is demonstrated by the fact that in the next five days, he and Jimmie Gaughan and Captain Williams, who was riding along in the Four Wheel Drive on a legless chair lashed to the side of the driver's seat, covered the remaining 230 miles to Atlanta four days and 75 miles ahead of the rest of the convoy.

"Captain Williams is a jolly good fellow," Dorn now wrote back to his sister.

> He wades right in with us. When we get stuck, we get out and shovel and push and chop down trees and lay them under the wheels. He always wears his uniform on the road. He weighs about two hundred and is all muscle. We average about eight to ten miles an hour.

On March 11, the Atlanta *Georgian and News* reported the arrival of Captain Williams, Frank Dorn, and Jimmie Gaughan in the Four Wheel Drive, noting that the Autocar was expected in that night and the White, waiting for repairs near Concord, the next day. Accompanying the report was a four-column, half-page photograph of the three men and the mud-laden truck. Better than any prose account it indicates the severity of the hazards the Four Wheel Drive had been through. Literally every part of the open truck carried a 6-inch coating of drying mud, covering hood, headlights, steering gear, driving levers, the bulbous side horn, and even the driver's seat. Dozens of times in an hour's driving, as Frank Dorn puts it today, "after hittin' them goddamn mudholes, I'd have to jam on the brakes and bring her to a stop while we all sat there cuppin' that goddamn yellow clay from our eyes and goggles."

To the readers of the Atlanta *Georgian and News* certainly one of the eye-catching features of the article was the four-column headline: "GASOLINE MAY BANISH ARMY MULE, GOVERNMENT TRUCK HERE ON TEST." That the mule traders and buyers and even farmers along the route were aware that the test run of motor vehicles might prove inimical to their own interests—the number of mules in the country then being well over four and one-half million, most of them raised and sold in the states through which the convoy was passing—is attested to by other factors. "The test is to determine whether trucks may be substituted for the four-mule teams that follow the army during regular engagements," the editor of the *Carolina Watchman* had written a few days earlier, though he had immediately reassured his readers "that the total abolition of mules is not contemplated at all." A similar uneasiness may have accounted for two other items in his report—the first an erroneous assertion that the test was being made at the request of motor companies who, according to him, furnished the trucks and paid for the expenses, and second, the rather heavy play given the fact that Captain Williams was a fellow North Carolinian from near Fayetteville, a graduate of West Point with high honors, and that he was being entertained at Charlotte by a lifelong friend, Captain J. A. Parker of the Hornets' Nest Riflemen.

That this, however, didn't allay the fears of the farmers along the road is indicated by an incident between Gaffney, South Carolina, and Atlanta. Moving along early one morning over the snow-covered roads, the White had suddenly dropped into soft mud up over the axles, front and rear, with only waste cotton fields along either side of the road and no trees or timber or telegraph poles to be used as traction material or as an anchor for the block and tackle. There was nothing left then but for the drivers to hunt up the nearest farmer half a mile away and ask for his mules.

"Consarn it, no!" the farmer growled. "Do you fellers think that's all I got to do? If them gover'ment fellers up to Washington got that much money and don't know what to do, they got to load up a bunch of these here automobiles with sand and send 'em down here to get stuck in the mud fer my mules to pull out, that's some gall. An' my mules ain't agoin' to either."

In laying out his plans for the test run, Captain Williams had figured on three weeks for the entire trip. By the time the convoy had reached Atlanta, they had been on the road for more than four and a half weeks, with roughly two-thirds of the total distance still to go. Fortunately the heavy spring rains were beginning to let up and the roads improved as the convoy turned northward. On the morning of March 16, the White having come in the day before, all three trucks, once more in convoy, left the city of Atlanta for Rome, Georgia. By the eighteenth the convoy had arrived at Chattanooga (75 miles above Rome), and on the nineteenth, 20 miles north of the city, crossed the Tennessee River, so swollen by the earlier rains that it was impossible to cross on the hand-operated ferry until Captain Williams procured the help of a launch from a nearby government project to tow the ferry safely across the stream.

From Chattanooga the route lay through the rough and muddy bottom lands and then up the mountains over an improved road maintained by a private corporation to Tracy

City. Between the latter and Beach Grove, the next stop, the convoy ran through 45 miles of mud and mire and around sinkholes deep enough so that only two days earlier a horse had actually been drowned in one of them before he could be unhitched from a wagon which had been stuck in the mud. From Beach Grove the route lay through Nashville to Bowling Green and then on to Magnolia, where the convoy rested on Sunday, March 25, and the men found worthy of report chiefly the menu—pork and biscuits on Saturday night, fat pork and big thick biscuits three times on Sunday, and pork and biscuits on Monday morning.

Throughout the states of Tennessee and Kentucky the issue of the army mule kept coming to the fore, though already on a note of half surrender. "AUTOS BEING TESTED FOR REPLACING ARMY MULES," a Chattanooga paper headlined its story:

> The poor brute that has been lambasted over many a muddy road and steep hillside, pulling wagon trains and carrying packs, and gaining thereby a notable place, not only among the heroes of past wars, but in the pages of history and literature as well, is about to give way at last in the march of progress to the automobile.

On the twenty-sixth the convoy reached the Government Depot at Jeffersonville, where the trucks took on some supplies ready to be shipped to Fort Benjamin Harrison, crossed the Ohio River into Louisville, and headed north for the last leg of the journey to the fort. Their troubles, however, were not yet over. Just below Crothersville, Indiana, as they hit a particularly bad stretch of open road, the mud once more piled up against the radiator and over the running boards until even the Four Wheel Drive had to give up for want of traction, and the three trucks were left sitting in the middle of the road, while the men scurried to a neighboring farmhouse for supper and afterward returned to an empty schoolhouse nearby, where they spent the night. At daylight the next morning, resorting once more to the block and tackle and the help of a telephone pole at the top of the hill, the men freed the vehicles and continued to Franklin. On the next and final day, the convoy reached Fort Benjamin Harrison, 1,509 miles from the starting point, seven weeks out of Washington, four weeks behind schedule.

For the War Department, Captain Williams had accumulated a mass of data useful later in the design and specifications of military vehicles. For the automobile and tire companies, he had kept accurate records of mileage, gasoline and oil consumption, the use of pneumatic as opposed to solid rubber tires, the relative superiority of different magnetos and carburetors. The longest day's run for the trip had been 98 miles; the shortest, 11. The average speed of forward movement for the entire trip had ranged between 8 and 10 miles per hour. The trucks had averaged between 4 and 5 miles per gallon of gasoline and roughly a hundred miles per gallon of oil.

For himself, Captain Williams had become convinced that "automobile trucks are cheaper, quicker and generally more advantageous from a military standpoint than mules and wagons." "They can be depended upon under any conditions where mules and wagons can be used," he had said back in Atlanta, and he now concluded his report to the quartermaster by writing, "I hope to see the motor trucks developed to such a state of efficiency . . . that it will be necessary to replace the mules and wagons." It is quite evident, however, that others, both within the Army and among laymen, were less sanguine.

In the April 20 issue of *Automobile Topics* the editor commented as follows:

> Wise old greybeards in the United States Army who have contended from the very beginning that nothing could ever equal in efficiency the army mule are still shaking their heads and chuckling over the results of the recently concluded test of motor trucks under army auspices. One of the four cars on trial had to be sent back to the factory, they point out, while the others were repeatedly mired and could be extricated only by the severest and most persistent labor. Surely this proves that the automobile will never, never do.

Captain Williams was relieved of his special assignment for the development of motor transportation with the Quartermaster Corps, shortly afterwards returned to his own regiment, the 19th Infantry, and left for a tour of duty in the Philippines.

For the Four Wheel Drive Auto Company the test run, with the markedly superior showing of its own product, confirmed its deepest conviction of the soundness and utility of the four-wheel-drive principle. It also confirmed Walter A. Olen's original conviction that the future of the company might lie in the trucking field. Of the seven pleasure cars originally planned, three were reconverted and sold as trucks, and though the Washington–Fort Harrison test run did not produce the influx of government orders that the directors had hoped for or the stockholders envisioned, it served at a crucial moment in the company's existence to give it a new direction and to steady the declining value of its shares.

The Great Goose Parade

With the news of the successful performance of the Four Wheel Drive on the test run, hope in Clintonville ran high. At last they were building a product that the world markets were clamoring for; it would only be a matter of months now, or weeks, or even days, until orders would pile in, trucks would roll out, ten, twenty, or even thirty a month. That would be nearly one a day, and down at Elermann's saloon they were even talking the fantastic figure of 500 a year—and the easy money and the profits that would accrue.

Joe Cotton gave the news a three-column spread in the *Tribune*, editorializing in his news column as he did so:

> A couple of weeks ago, in speaking of the magnificent Christmas gifts other cities were heralding in the way of public improvements and new industries, we intimated that while this city had no such rosy hues as a Christmas offering, prospects were decidedly bright for a New Year's gift that would be the best in Clintonville's history. The promised day has come and every citizen of this community will rejoice and all stockholders in the now famous

Four Wheel Drive Auto Company will be especially elated to learn that Uncle Sam has stepped to the front and places his stamp of approval on the Four Wheel Drive cars made at Clintonville.

Similar sentiment, mingled with echoes of envy and regret, appeared in the papers of neighboring towns, at Green Bay, Appleton, Marion, New London, Manawa, Hartford, and Shawano. "Antigo missed another golden opportunity," opined the editor of the *Daily Journal;* "the Four Wheel Drive Auto factory is putting Clintonville on the map and the factory is as yet barely started." "The people of Fond du Lac turned down an opportunity to place their municipality among the foremost cities in the automobile world," wrote a Fond du Lac editor. "Clintonville has something uncommonly good, immeasurably rich in the future," wrote the editor of the Wittenberg *Enterprise;* "looks to us like Clintonville will some day have a plant that will cover acres where it now covers square rods."

The current rumor in Clintonville was that the government was about to buy 1,200 vehicles, and expectations soared. For a week or two there was lively talk of buying and subscribing for stock, and for the first time since the company had been organized, a man could sell back what he had subscribed for at something approaching par value.

But the government orders did not follow. To be sure the Army was still interested, but the mills of brass grind slowly. Shortly after the purchase of the original touring-car chassis, the Quartermaster Corps expressed an interest in a 3-ton truck, designed especially and geared down to haul heavy supplies in the field, and the spring months at the factory were spent in designing and building the truck according to Army specifications. The activities of P. J. F. Batenburg, factory superintendent and chief engineer, and of the machinists and workmen were feverish. Walter A. Olen gave his full time and attention to promotion and the sale of stock. In May the new truck was ready for delivery, and the Army, still unconvinced, had set up a new test run.

For this trial the War Department proposed a march of 260 miles from Dubuque, Iowa, to Sparta, Wisconsin, by a provisional regiment, using both motorized vehicles and mules as a means of transportation. For the new test the three trucks used on the earlier run, the White, the Sampson, and the Four Wheel Drive were brought out to Dubuque from Fort Benjamin Harrison. In addition the government also rented three 1½-ton trucks, a Kelly Springfield, a Mack, and a Kato, assigning one to each of the six companies in the regiment, where they were to replace four-mule escort wagons on the daily march. To haul supplies for the regiment from the base depots, a service usually supplied by rail, the War Department authorized the rental of six 3-ton trucks, each from one of six different truck manufacturers, at a rental of $12 a day, including drivers and repairs. It was in the latter competition that the newly designed 3-ton Four Wheel Drive was entered. Chauncey Williams and Frank Dorn accompanied it as drivers, while the management and engineers of the various companies were invited as observers.

Competition among the various companies, and between the mule escort wagons and trucks, was severe. All the light trucks were overloaded; the soft roads were cut into shreds by the narrow rims of the army wagons; forced to slow down to the gait of foot soldiers, the trucks overheated and stalled easily. On the second day out of Dubuque the Kelly Springfield developed motor trouble and was withdrawn, all of the others, however, coming through to Madison with the help of mules and the Four Wheel Drive, which was taken "out of the column on the second day and used to pull the other trucks out of sand and mud and get them back on the road."

The 3-ton trucks hauling provisions and supplies had similar difficulties. The bakery remained at Dubuque until the regiment was within 30 miles of Madison, Wisconsin, and the trucks had to make 80 miles daily with loads of provisions to the regimental camping place. The bakery moved to Madison only when the auto trucks failed to make the distance, which forced the regiment to fall back on emergency supplies. While the regiment made its way from Madison to Sparta, a distance of 130 miles, the bakery remained at Madison and continued to turn out six hundred 4-pound loaves of bread daily. These were carried overland with thirty sacks of oats and 2,000 pounds of beef or bacon by the auto trucks until the troops were within 50 miles of Sparta. That any trucks managed to survive the ordeal in the heavy-clay and sandy roads was remarkable and that the Four Wheel Drive outperformed the others was attested to by all the regimental officers accompanying the march.

It was also attested to by the competition among the drivers. Tampering with the motor of a rival truck was frequent, and after an early experience on the road to Madison, Williams and Dorn took turns sleeping on a tarpaulin under the front wheels of the truck. The drivers, with their heavily loaded trucks, trying to outmaneuver each other, subjected the vehicles to impossible hazards of sand and mire, tearing

ABOVE: The Zachow and Besserdich Machine Shop, where the original four-wheel-drive invention was hammered out on a blacksmith's anvil.

BELOW: Earliest Four Wheel Drive Auto Company building, where the factory whistle blew for the first time on December 20, 1911.

Otto Zachow, machinist and blacksmith, inventor of the first successful four-wheel-drive motor vehicle, prototype of the later jeep. "No one who knew him ever doubted his word."

Walter A. Olen, Clintonville attorney, under whose organizing genius the company grew in eight years from the smallest to the then largest manufacturer of four-wheel-drive trucks. "Hire people who can do something better than you can, and then make it easy for them to do it the way you want it done."

OPPOSITE: The first completed Four Wheel Drive car, later christened the *Battleship*. "It surely is a dandy, deep maroon in color, large and roomy, holding eight people all told—two in front, four in the rear, and two on folding seats."

The arrival at Atlanta: Frank Dorn, Captain A. E. Williams, and Jimmie Gaughan. "A bunch of inexperienced government greenhorns trying to drive three trucks through acres of bottomless red clay. They have had three weeks of solid rain here and the cars sink out of sight in the mud."

OPPOSITE: In 1942 Captain A. E. Williams and Frank Dorn, earliest company driver, talk over the 1,600 miles of mud and mire of the U.S. Army test run in 1912. "When we get stuck, we get out and shovel and push and chop down trees and lay them under the wheels."

On the Dubuque to Sparta test run. "That any trucks managed to survive the ordeal in the heavy-clay and sandy roads was remarkable and that the Four Wheel Drive outperformed the others was attested to by all the regimental officers accompanying the march."

P. J. F. Batenburg, Dutch immigrant engineer, later
factory superintendent, joined the company
from 1911 to 1918. A prodigious worker and an
exacting taskmaster, his favorite remark, "The
faster it goes, the better how is it," still echoes
within the factory walls.

The first Four Wheel Drive 3-ton truck, built for the
Dubuque to Sparta test run, tries out the clay
streets of Clintonville.

OPPOSITE: The Four Wheel Drive, Model B, of World
War I. "They were found everywhere, hurrying
supplies of all descriptions where most needed and
at the right time, frequently turning the tide of battle."

A 50-truck train of FWD's leaving the
factory for the port of embarkation
in World War I.

Farewell to the city of Clintonville,
We bid thee a fond adieu;
We may go to hell in an FWD,
But we'll never come back to you.

"You couldn't wear them out and you couldn't tear them apart . . . the ride was like that of a rough, bucking bronco, but they burrowed down like six yoke of oxen and you could never tire the damn things out."

ABOVE: The first contingent of Model B's in World War I. "The British order hit the city of Clintonville like a circle wind."

Chauncey Williams, company driver, eluding a challenger in the Buelow gravel pit in 1912.

Luella Bates, company test driver, at the New York Auto Show in 1920. "Miss Bates weighed only 130 pounds, but dressed in an Oxford-gray uniform, puttees, and a jaunty overseas cap, she could handle the 3-ton truck as if it were a tricycle."

The Four Wheel Drive race car at Indianapolis with
Mauri Rose at the wheel. "I want to say that I have
never driven a car or a truck that had the safety of
steering or the traction to compare with a Four Wheel
Drive car."

through, daring others to follow, or at other times forcing a rival truck into an impassable stretch. On one occasion, too, with the big Four Wheel Drive parked along the street on a slope and the drivers resting under the shade of a tree on the opposite side of the street, the brakes were mysteriously released and the big truck went crashing down into a bridge, damaging the front axle and radiator.

To some degree, certainly, the rival companies helped to defeat each other, though even without such antics, two fundamental problems remained: the almost impassable condition of the early roads during a greater portion of the year, and the necessity for gearing down motor vehicles accompanying the troops to a mile and a half an hour, the forward progress of a foot army. In spite of the commendation of officers in the field for the four-wheel-drive principle, all the rented trucks were discharged as soon as the regiment reached Sparta, and Williams and Dorn drove the Four Wheel Drive back to Clintonville.

With the failure of the government to follow through on the expected order for 1,200 vehicles, gloom settled over the town and the factory. To be sure, the men were kept busy, and as the summer progressed more and more of the individual cars and trucks already under construction were completed and sold. The first car had gone to August Matuzczak; the second, to Marcus Model, proprietor of the Ward House, for whom it had been reconverted into a bus, hauling passengers from the depot the three-quarters of a mile to the hotel. The third and fourth touring cars were now completed and sold, one to M. W. Pinkerton of the Pinkerton Detective Agency of Chicago and the second to Charles W. Zingler of Shiocton.

Even more auspicious for the future of the company was the sale of a touring-car chassis contracted for by the Lincoln Park Commission of Chicago early in March, since the truck foreshadowed the enormous development of the motor truck for use in highway maintenance. Designed for the maintenance of the concrete highways within the park, the truck, powered with a 30-horsepower gasoline motor, geared down to run from 1 to 10 miles per hour, was equipped with an 8-foot cylinder of revolving brushes, mounted at the front of the truck and driven by an auxiliary motor on the rear of the chassis. This was to keep the streets free of snow. In the summertime the brushes were to be removed and a 14,000-gallon water tank and flushing pump mounted on the chassis for the flushing of streets. The estimate was that the truck would replace eight teams and twenty-four men. In October, too, another truck was delivered to the United States government, this one for testing and use as an ambulance by the Medical Corps.

The first commercial sale of the 3-ton truck, specifically developed for government use in the Dubuque-to-Sparta test, was to the Silver City Beer and Ice Company of Denver. Other 1½-ton trucks and 3-ton trucks sold later on during that year and well into the next went chiefly to pickle and canning companies, and to breweries in Appleton, Green Bay, and Milwaukee, though the latter sales met with public opposition. In the spring of 1913 the Appleton *Post* carried a bitter complaint to the city commissioners on the part of residents of the city, because the Four Wheel Drive truck operating for the Appleton Brew and Malt Company had been cutting down through the frozen surface to a depth of 6 to 10 inches and churning the streets into a mire, a condition certainly uncomfortable to the pedestrian and the horse-drawn vehicle, though not without its compliment to the sturdy power of the motor truck.

In spite of the intermittent sales, however, the prospects of the company steadily declined. Costs of inventory and materials kept mounting. The sale of stock, the one way of assuring the necessary capital to meet the increasing cost of materials and labor, grew more sluggish. The original capitalization of the company at $110,000 had been largely subscribed for, though it had netted little enough cash at the prevailing rate of 25 per cent down, the stockholder inevitably trusting to profits and dividends to pay out the rest. In July of 1911 the capitalization had been increased to $250,000, but much of the new stock remained to be sold. With the failure or at least the delay of the U.S. Army in coming through with the anticipated order, this proved difficult.

The surest way to arouse interest in the company was to send out its product with the factory drivers, Frank Dorn and Chauncey Williams. During the summers of 1912 and 1913 the two men, singly or working together, toured practically the entire state, demonstrating in every village or town of any size. In June of the second year, when the town of Clintonville entertained a special trainload of merchants and manufacturers from Milwaukee, the entire group, including the famous Harvester Band, was taken out to the Buelow gravel pit, where Chauncey "drove the car around the sand dunes, climbed a grade of fifty-four per cent to a shelf the length of the car and from there made a leap drive into the pit, a drop of over eight feet, the front wheels being at least four feet in the air when the rear wheels left the edge of the shelf," a stunt compared to the Vanderbilt Cup race or the Grand Prix by the visitors. Later on in the same summer one of the trucks was driven from Clintonville to New York City, demonstrating in the larger cities along the route.

But the shares still moved slowly. Special agents, selling stock on commission, were employed. Walter A. Olen began a two-year-long campaign of selling by personal letter, writing to hundreds and even thousands of bankers and professional men throughout the country. To expedite the payment of stock on the part of those who had already subscribed, the board of directors authorized cash assessments against them, as well as directing the general manager and president to bring court suits. Fortunately for the future of the company, such action was again and again deferred. It was difficult enough to sell new shares at $110 per share when subscribed stock in Clintonville was being sold back to the company for $50 per share, but certainly nothing would have killed the company more quickly than a suit against its own stockholders, whatever the paid or unpaid amount. The secret was, in the face of bankruptcy, to sell sufficient stock to preclude the possibility, or to sell stock at its par value to save values already well declined below par. So stringent had affairs become by the summer of 1913 that stock was privately changing hands at less than half of its par value, and in one case when the board of directors offered to buy back a share of stock at $50, it did so, though since there was no ready cash available, it acted merely as an agent to resell it at the same price to one of its directors, Charles Hagen.

Earlier in the summer, when the prospects for a U.S. Army order were brighter, the manager and board of directors had once more resorted to an earlier maneuver—the threat of moving the plant out of Clintonville. Appleton seemed a likely choice, and W. A. Olen had succeeded in interesting a group of Appleton businessmen under the leadership of John Conway, the owner and proprietor of the leading hotel. Early in July a mass meeting of citizens in Appleton had voted to try to raise a subscription of $100,000, provided that the plant was moved and the company would permit an examination of its books by an expert auditor to determine the real state of its affairs. At the annual meeting of the stockholders in Clintonville on July 13 a committee from Appleton presented their proposition and were overwhelmingly turned down, an endorsement that served well to boost the city and company morale—though without adding much to its coffers.

When neither the sale of stock nor the profits from the cars and trucks completed and sold were sufficient to meet expenses, the company resorted to borrowing. As early as October the board of directors had authorized the president to negotiate a loan of $3,500 for sixty days. In November of the same year the company sought a loan of $10,000 from the State Bank of Clintonville, offering to secure it with a mortgage on plant and property. Within the next three months the company again resorted to borrowing, this time $5,000 with the members of the board of directors each going as surety and taking a lien on trucks in various stages of manufacture, a procedure repeated again and again during the next two years. In retrospect it is difficult to understand how the company actually survived. To build five 3-ton trucks the company would have to order the materials, borrowing the money to do so. To pay the workmen and to meet running expenses it would have to mortgage to the directors the materials of the unfinished trucks. With the trucks completed and sold, the loans would have to be repaid and the actual profits dispersed as interest and current expenses. And then the whole procedure would have to be gone through again. It is almost inconceivable that a company capitalized at $250,000 was frequently doing business on a margin of considerably less than $1,000.

Something needs to be said for the courage and determination of the president and general manager and for the stanch support of the board of directors. Walter A. Olen was by nature buoyant and optimistic; but to launch, in a little town of fewer than 2,000 inhabitants, an industry needing a capitalization of $250,000 and largely dependent on that local support, while at the same time grappling for world markets in competition with established truck manufacturers, demanded a singleness of purpose and tenacity, a sleepless vigilance, the naïveté of a yet undefeated entrepreneur, coupled with the persuasive skill of an old-time religious exhorter. When it was a matter of selling stock or persuading the citizens of Clintonville not to relinquish the factory, he was ready to address a mass meeting. If there was a rumor in the truck industry that the Federal government might be interested, he was off to Washington, D.C., talking to the quartermaster general of the United States Army. In any public demonstration of the Four Wheel Drive truck, he was more than likely to be riding the front seat alongside the driver. During the early years he supervised the sale of practically every truck or car that left the factory. He wrote the advertising. It was he who cajoled the bankers into extending loans, signing the liens on unfinished trucks to see them through to completion.

In the midst of the most difficult straits, he saw that if the company was to survive, it needed to expand, to build more trucks, to meet more markets, to enlarge its plant capacity in terms of floor space and machinery. In the summer of 1912, for instance, in a doubtful moment with the Army holding off and the domestic market as yet completely uncertain, he persuaded the board of directors to increase the plant by adding a new building, to order materials for ten new trucks, to set aside $2,000 for advertising, and to approve the printing and issuing of 10,000 catalogues. He and the board of directors, as he saw it, were in business for the entire community, and his own position was in a sense one of public trust. The company could not—did not dare to—fail.

But there were innumerable problems. The original patents for the ball-and-socket steering joint as well as for the subtransmission which distributed power equally to front and rear axles had long since been cleared and granted, but there was always, of course, the problem and danger of other companies infringing upon the patents. There was also a danger of infringing upon the patent rights of others. At the time the original patents had been granted, the Selden patents, though contested, were still in force, and practically the entire automobile industry, with the exception of Henry Ford, the contestant, was paying a license for the manufacture of any self-propelled road vehicle powered by a gasoline engine. There were other patents, covering a conventional transmission and the radius rods running from the transmission to the rear axle, which brought claims of infringement against the company totaling more than a million dollars. By 1910, however, the Selden patents had been declared invalid by the United States Circuit Court of Appeals, and the infringement of patents covering the transmission and radius rods cleared through the development of a jaw-clutch transmission and an adaptation of the Hotchkiss drive through the front and rear axle springs.

To investigate the possibility that the original ball-and-socket patent might be open to claims of infringement by an inventor in a neighboring state, Mr. Olen visited the town, posing as a landholder and real-estate operator in northern Wisconsin. He talked to the local banker and others and finally persuaded a local realtor to drive him out to the village where the inventor lived. There he viewed the invention and talked to the inventor about a factory in Clintonville currently involved, so he had heard, in building a four-wheel-drive truck. The inventor was skeptical but interested, though later when the Clintonville firm to avoid any future trouble offered him $25,000 for his invention through a third party, the offer was turned down, the inventor thinking—as many a man does—that if his invention was worth that much to others, it would be worth a lot more to him.

There were other problems. If the company was to sell its product on a national market and to compete with other motor companies, there were branch agencies to be established. There were new markets for the motor-truck industry to be discovered and explored. The highway sweeper and sprinkler for the Lincoln Park Commission of Chicago had been one such. Late in the summer of 1912, P. J. F. Batenburg was busy designing a fire truck for the city of Minneapolis. There were foreign markets to be thought of.

Largely because of the publicity attendant upon the successful performance of the Four Wheel Drive car in the Washington–Fort Benjamin Harrison test run, a 1½-ton truck had been shipped to São Paulo, Brazil. There would be other foreign markets as well.

By the end of the fiscal year of 1913, somehow the company had weathered its most severe crisis. In 1911 they had built and sold one car. In 1912 they had completed six touring-car chassis and manufactured three 1½- and two 3-ton trucks. In 1913 they had built five 1½-ton trucks and fourteen 3-ton trucks. But they had been in business now for nearly four years and there were still no profits and no dividends. Stock was changing hands through company approval at prices ranging from $50 to $75. Of the money due for stock subscribed for, nearly $50,000 remained unpaid. To encourage the reluctant stockholders, the board of directors agreed that henceforth, on each vehicle sold, $500 might be set aside for the payment of future dividends and that at any rate a $4-per-share dividend on all paid-up stock be declared payable by July 1. But no one in Clintonville at that moment could foresee what the next year was to bring.

Suddenly in the summer of 1914 the conflict in Europe broke into open war on the battlefield, and with the German invasion of Belgium, the collapse of forts at Liége, Namur, and Maubeuge, and the drive toward Paris, there was a feverish demand on the part of the combatants to avail themselves of American productivity and a ready response on the part of American exporters to avail themselves of the new markets. Among the modern weapons of war the motor was just coming into its own, in the dirigible balloon, in the airplane, and in the motorcar. But while these were in successful use largely in scouting and reconnoitering, the motor truck itself was available for actual conflict, the hauling of supplies, the moving of artillery, and even the transportation of the troops themselves. Here was an immediate use for thousands of trucks, and in the open terrain of the battlefield none would be so successful as a truck capable of pulling itself along on all four wheels.

Walter A. Olen was himself aware of the possibilities, but there were difficulties involved. How could the Four Wheel Drive truck of Clintonville enter the European conflict? How could they ship trucks to England and France? How make contacts? Mr. Olen wrote to the embassies and consulates. When Bethlehem Steel, which had contracts with the governments of France and England, invited the motor companies to demonstrate their products, the Four Wheel Drive Auto Company entered the competition. At the fenced-in yard at Bethlehem, Pennsylvania, the Four Wheel Drive truck displayed its prowess by climbing a grade of 49 per cent up a stair of lumber piled as high as a second-story window. In the field test the truck drove across a plowed field of 10-inch-deep mud into an open ditch with 22-inch perpendicular walls and then up a steep 60-foot hill, but, as Mr. Olen feared, nothing came of it, since there were too many rivals, the competition was fierce, and the original five-percenters had taken over.

In the end, acting on his own hunch, Mr. Olen accompanied by Mr. Batenburg went to New York City and succeeded in interesting the export firm of Gaston, Williams and Wigmore in the possibility of the truck abroad. Late in the fall of 1914 the company sold two trucks to the exporters at wholesale, a 3-ton and a 5-ton, to be shipped to

England, the company agreeing to send along a driver and a company salesman, the export firm to meet all other expenses. Within four weeks the trucks had arrived and been tested, and the first order for fifty trucks had been cabled back to the factory. The order hit the city of Clintonville like a circle wind. Fifty trucks were more than the factory had produced in its entire history, and the order called for delivery in forty days.

What they needed first of all was $200,000 of working capital. To secure it, the company mortgaged the plant and buildings for $100,000, and Walter A. Olen once more went up and down the street seeking loans of $2,000 per truck, offering a chattel mortgage on the unbuilt trucks and 8 per cent interest for a ninety-day loan. Twenty-five thousand dollars had to be spent for new machinery. Before the first order of trucks was completed, the factory capacity had to be doubled again and a new building added to the plant. Before the last trucks of the first order had been built and loaded on the flatcars en route for New York, other orders had followed, and by the end of the next year, 288 three-ton Model B's had been shipped to England and another eighty-eight to Petrograd, with a backlog of orders from European countries for 200 trucks a month, a demand so insistent that Gaston, Williams and Wigmore suggested the company authorize a contract with the Peerless Automobile Company to build Four Wheel Drive trucks with royalties to the home company.

Suddenly the little factory in Clintonville had arrived. By the end of that year, 1915, the cash dividend rose to $30 per share, $4,000 was set aside for the depreciation of machinery, $9,000 for contingent funds, taxes, and commissions, and a stock dividend of 100 per cent was granted, automatically raising the capitalization of the company to $500,000. President Olen was voted a $1,000 bonus and his yearly salary raised to $3,000 per year. The price of the stock had risen to $150 per share, and all stock subscribed for but remaining unpaid was canceled and the money refunded. On the morning of November 26, as the factory whistle blew for the noon hour, 450 employees lined up in Automobile Row, facing the factory gates, as four large FWD's pulled up, loaded with 450 live geese. As the geese were distributed, one goose per man, the FWD band broke in and, heading the parade, led the workers, geese slung shoulderward, up to Main Street, through the business section of the city, south to the Congregational church, and back down to the city hall. As Joe Cotton noted for the record,

> It was a grand sight, a most wonderful thing in the history of our little city and one which will remain in our memories for years to come, and one which will be handed down to posterity as the Great Goose Parade of the Four Wheel Drive Auto Company.

For the little town of Clintonville it was indeed a happy Thanksgiving.

"For Wonderful Delivery" CHAPTER FIVE

With nearly 400 trucks built and shipped during the year 1915 and with a standing order from the Allied Governments for 200 trucks a month, the Four Wheel Drive Auto Company seemed well assured of its future. The January meeting of the stockholders was characterized as a "love-feast," the most harmonious one ever held. "Think of it," Joe Cotton wrote the next morning, "a million dollar corporation located in what was considered a short time ago as a nice, quiet little city . . . dependent chiefly upon the farmers of the neighborhood." Four years ago they had had a dream, one car finished, five in the process of manufacture, one truck ready for delivery to the United States Army; now they had built and sold more than 400 trucks, not to the Army as they had once anticipated, but all over the world, to England and France, to Russia, to Spain and to Portugal, to Brazil and to Argentina. It was an auspicious beginning, and with 200 a month on order, the future was indeed promising.

There also were, of course, problems. One of them was the constant need for increasing the manufacturing facilities. The factory buildings had already been enlarged three times. The stockholders were cautious by nature. Having waited four years for a return on their money and always somewhat dubious about the new venture, now that the money was actually coming in, they thought of little except sharing the profits. The directors themselves were caught in the middle. P. J. F. Batenburg clamored for buildings and materials. "I wish you could strike over your big hearts," he addressed the directors, "and allow us $25,000 for new equipment." In January the directors agreed, and a new stock-room building, heavy-duty turning lathes, milling machinery, boring bars, and drill presses, as well as a new heat-treating and tempering room, were added. In February, still hampered by their own inadequate facilities, the board of directors authorized Gaston, Williams and Wigmore to go ahead with the proposed contract with Peerless Auto Company for the manufacture of 500 trucks, with royalties to the home company, and authorized the first 100 to be ready by the first of October. In March the board of directors received an offer, which they were later to submit to the assembled stockholders, to sell out the company, lock, stock, and barrel, for $2,500,000.

But the success of 1915 was merely a prelude. On February 25, 1916, the United States government recognized General Carranza as president of Mexico. On March 8 and 9 came Villa's raid across the Rio Grande on the little town of Columbus, New Mexico, with the death of fourteen American soldiers and ten civilians. On March 10 President Wilson ordered General Pershing to the scene, and on March

15 Pershing crossed the border with a punitive force of 15,000 men to hunt down and disperse the bandits and to capture Villa. It was a difficult assignment for the Army. The 500-mile raid, 200 miles into the interior of Mexico, through the Chihuahua desert, was the kind of rapid maneuver for which the Army was ill-equipped in terms of transportation and supply, particularly since the Carranza government, suspicious of any foreign army on its soil, refused the right to use the railroad from Juárez to Casa Grande and since Pershing's orders had been to respect the sovereignty of Mexico by not occupying towns or living off the land.

It had been four years since the War Department had first experimented with the use of the Four Wheel Drive and other trucks in the Washington–Fort Benjamin Harrison run. Other experiments with the FWD, the Jeffery, the White, and the Packard had taken place at Fort Leavenworth, at Forts Sill and Riley, and at San Diego, but the Army had been searching for a standard design, and the emergency now caught them still ill equipped. The result was a demand on the truck companies for an immediate supply.

The first order from the United States Quartermaster Corps to the Four Wheel Drive Auto Company came on April 6 and called for 147 trucks, with drivers and mechanics, the first shipment to Columbus, New Mexico, to go in a fortnight. It was an impossible task. Since its full facilities for manufacture were already taxed to meet the European demand, the company had no reserve trucks on supply. Hastily the board of directors convened. A shipment of 44 trucks, already painted lead color for shipment to England, were being loaded into waiting boxcars on the factory siding. A wire to Washington asked for a four-week delay on the order. When the return came, asking for and even demanding immediate shipment under the National Defense Act, the trucks were unloaded, the paint scraped off, and a new coat of olive green for the U.S. Army was applied. The British Embassy at Washington was notified of the company's inability to ship on schedule. A wire from the British Ambassador at Washington, however, demanded immediate shipment. At this juncture, W. A. Olen left for Washington, where a settlement among the three parties was effected, and the trucks, once more recognized as England's property, were again unloaded, the paint rescraped, and a new coat of lead color applied, in preparation for their shipment abroad.

At the factory the work on the government order of trucks became feverish. The first big order from the U.S. Army was on hand, and though it was not so large as had earlier been anticipated, the company was eager to meet the requirement. The first shipment now called for twenty-eight trucks and forty trained drivers and mechanics to accompany them. Not only was it necessary to include the trucks in an already overloaded manufacturing schedule, but it was also necessary to recruit and to train the drivers and mechanics. The first shipment was finally ready on May 19. All afternoon the loading into the boxcars proceeded, though it wasn't until midnight that the moment of departure came. Then, with the company band playing, and hundreds of townsfolk cheering and waving good-by to the drivers and mechanics, the train pulled out.

A second carload of trucks left on June 23; a third, fourth, and fifth trainload left later on in the summer. Down in Mexico, General Pershing, with two troops of the 12th Cavalry, had penetrated as far as Parral, 400 miles south of the line, though later on during the summer he withdrew his main forces as far as Colonia Dublan, where headquarters were established. Throughout the entire march the procurement and delivery of supplies had depended upon trucks. Over the difficult terrain 7,000 feet above sea level, through the intense cold in the mountains and the hot winds of the desert, over rock cliffs and boulder-strewn passes, through the drifting sands and the axle-deep mud of the valleys, the trucks had labored to supply the men. Before the summer was over, 4,000 trucks and cars of various makes had been used in the expedition, but they had been cars and trucks designed for the relatively good roads of America, and most of them were now driven by inexperienced men and the shipments had been accompanied with insufficient spare parts. Both cars and trucks had played their part, but they had left a trail through the Mexican desert of broken springs, burned-out engines, bent frames, and worn-out tires. By the time the U.S. Army forces were finally withdrawn, 2,000 trucks were out of commission and had been left abandoned to the winds and sands of the mountains and desert.

The FWD's had come through singularly well, a fact not only attested to by the drivers and mechanics, like Joe Stein and Ward Winchester, accompanying the expedition, but also by the Army officers, including Captain Williams, who testified in his official reports that "the FWD is proving its superiority to all others in the Mexican service." By January 18 of the next year the company had shipped another trainload of trucks to Honolulu, and the 8th Regiment of

Artillery became the first unit of the United States Army to be completely equipped with motor transportation. Full equipment included thirty Holt tractors for guns, three motorcycles for scouting, one Ford truck equipped with rapid-fire light weapons, and thirty-six FWD's for supplies and ammunition, including one machine-shop truck, equipped with a forge and lathes and drill presses to keep the others in repair.

But even this, in terms of what was to follow, was only a beginning. Early in the next spring the conflict raging on the continent of Europe engulfed America, and on April 8 the United States Congress declared war upon Germany. The reality of the conflict had, of course, for some time been drawing nearer and nearer, even to the inhabitants of Clintonville, lost in the midcontinent area. Throughout 1916 there had been increasing numbers of European representatives in town from France and England and from Russia. Since early in 1916 Lieutenant Cleaver from the British Army had inspected and passed 720 trucks. One shipment of seven trucks for the Russians had fallen into the hands of the Germans when the *Suchan,* bound for Archangel, had been captured in the Arctic Ocean, east of Cape North. Another shipment had gone down off the Strait of Gibraltar as a result of submarine warfare. More than once a trainload of trucks, bound for Britain, had been tampered with between the factory and the point of embarkation by German agents and sympathizers, who had emptied emery into the crankcases or worked fine stone and resin into the transmissions and differentials or poured camphor and gummy liquids into the gas tanks. But even so the sentiment and sympathies of Clintonville were divided.

On April 3, with the war seemingly imminent and in anticipation of the Act of Congress, W. A. Olen had called a meeting of the board of directors. Should not the company, remembering its earlier difficulties, in the case of war cancel its European contracts and place its entire output at the disposal of the United States government? For a moment there was strong dissension. Half the members of the board were of German descent, the sons of immigrants, with friends and kinfolk still in Europe. They were not disloyal Americans, but, their parents having left their homeland because of internecine strife, they were doubtful of either the necessity or the advisability of America's entering the conflict, a feeling that still prevails in some parts of the state. Moreover, as other members of the board suggested, would it not mean cutting themselves off from the European markets which had really given them their first real start? And what about the domestic markets—the oil wells, the lumbering industry, the transport field—just becoming interested and upon which they would ultimately depend for their peacetime sales?

On the other hand the country was clearly in danger. The Four Wheel Drive trucks had proved their superiority in the field of military supply not only in Europe but in Mexico. The people of Clintonville, divided in their sentiments, needed the boost in morale which such an action would bring to them. It would serve to unite them as citizens of their own community, and of the state of Wisconsin, and of the country itself.

The patriotic sentiment prevailed. On the afternoon of the third, a wire was sent to the Secretary of War, Newton D. Baker:

The Board of Directors of this Company unanimously tender the output of the Four Wheel Drive Auto Company to the United States upon such terms as may be satisfactory to the War Department, and subject only to existing contracts, foreign and domestic.

The reply did not arrive until the fifteenth. "Gentlemen," it read,

Your telegram of 5 April has been brought to my attention and Senator Husty has also called my attention to the generous offer which your company has made to the government. As a matter of business, this will be referred to the Quartermaster General for his consideration, but I cannot allow the opportunity to pass without expressing my appreciation of your generous and patriotic action.

The order for trucks did not arrive until July, but it called for the largest quantity of trucks that had ever been ordered by the United States Army from any single manufacturer, 3,750 three-ton trucks to be delivered at the rate of 175 trucks a month, for a total cost of $12,000,000.

For the little company that had started five years earlier it was not only an opportunity, but also an almost overwhelming obligation. The output of the factory would have to be tripled. New employees would have to be recruited and trained. Hastily the board of directors let contracts for three new buildings, and sent out order after order for new machines and tools to be installed in them. The recruiting of workers was more difficult, since the labor supply of the city was limited. Men from the neighboring farms and outlying villages, from Shiocton and Embarrass and Manawa and even as far away as Antigo, were induced to come in to supply the need. But this brought its own problems of transportation, housing, and entertainment. The board of directors called upon the city to build 200 new houses and offered to finance any private builders who would go ahead and erect homes for its workers. It appropriated $5,000 to erect a boardinghouse for its commuters and organized a Goodfellowship Club of more than 100 workers to provide clubrooms for the commuting workers, with facilities for use in leisure time, for reading, letter writing, and games. "Men are more vital to the success of an enterprise than money," Mr. Olen declared publicly.

> We need men, many men, men with new ideas, men with executive and organizing ability, and with patience to wait for the reward of their efforts . . . the success of an institution or a community is not dependent upon a few exceptional men but is based on the faithfulness and loyalty and the integrity of the average workers.

In addition to the trucks to be manufactured there were the drivers and mechanics to be trained. By November the Ordnance Department of the United States Army took over this project, supplying its own soldier drivers and mechanics and establishing a training school under the leadership of Captain Herning. To house the men to be trained in the thirty-day school, the government erected a barracks on the rising slope west of the factory. Early in December the flag-raising ceremony for the new building took place with the marching band from the factory escorting the workers, the speaker, the Honorable E. R. Hicks of Oshkosh, and the contingent of 180 enlisted men and thirty officers, from the Northwestern Station to the Ward House for lunch, and then on to the barracks for the public ceremony.

A week or so later, the public spirit of the town having

risen to new heights with the presence of the soldiers, the women of Clintonville organized a Welfare Club for the young soldier trainees at the newly erected I.O.O.F. Hall, where literary and musical programs were held. Joe Cotton described it eloquently:

> Here is initiative, the gentility that knows not affectation, the education that teaches democracy, the accomplishments, the social graces . . . the selected men, the flower of the country's manhood, chivalrous sons from nearly all states meeting the fair flowers of beauty from Clintonville's teeming gardens of life.

It was no wonder that on the day in January, 1918, when the first contingent was ready to leave the city at the end of its training period, as the men gathered at the Northwestern Station with their newly made friends, one of the soldiers climbed a nearby telephone pole and called upon the assembled crowd for "three cheers for the city of Clintonville and its fair ladies."

In July, the original order for trucks having been tripled, the number of trainees from the Ordnance Department rose to 1,500 men, who on the completion of their training were assigned to drive truck trains overland from Clintonville to the point of embarkation at Baltimore, gathering supplies and equipment en route. The number of men had long since outstripped the capacity of the barracks, and most of them had been housed in a tent colony farther up on the hill to the west and north of the factory, where the summer rains and heat and the blizzards of a Wisconsin winter were equally discomforting. It was not surprising that one of the last contingents to leave in the heavy winter of 1918, a group of Southerners from the states of Georgia and South Carolina, should have celebrated their departure by pinning a scroll of paper to the dining-room table top with a bayonet. "To the City of Clintonville," it read:

> Farewell to the city of Clintonville,
> We bid thee a fond adieu;
> We may go to hell in an FWD,
> But we'll never come back to you.

There were many public-spirited occasions. In October the second Liberty Loan drive had been opened in the Folkman Opera House with an address by attorney Paul Winters of Shawano to an overflowing crowd. The goal had been set for $50,000 in Clintonville. The city subscribed $101,300. The third Liberty Loan, early in April on the anniversary of the declaration of war, was launched with factory whistles blowing and church bells ringing, and with a parade of soldiers and scouts, closing three weeks later with a parade of factory workers, led by the factory band, and followed by 200 officers and men and a contingent of newly completed FWD trucks. The quota for the loan had been $43,000. The city had actually subscribed $183,000.

By the middle of the summer of 1918 the factory had produced nearly 10,000 trucks for the United States government and its allies, and so insistent had the demand become for the FWD's that the War Department in contract with the Four Wheel Drive Auto Company had licensed the Premier Motor Corporation of Indianapolis, the Mitchell Motor Car Company of Racine, and the Kissel Motor Corporation of Hartford, Wisconsin, to build the truck, the home company to exchange patent rights, patterns, and drawings for a $200 royalty per truck. Of the 10,000 trucks, more than half were already on the battlefields of Europe, where the motor truck, like the machine gun and the airplane and later the tank, was drastically changing the character of war and battlefield maneuver.

The forte of the military truck in the First World War lay in supply. Neither artillery nor infantry had as yet been motorized so as to permit rapid strategic or tactical maneuver, and with the development of the machine gun the battlefield had assumed the basic principle of siege or trench warfare. At the first battle of the Marne, however, General Joffre had already indicated the strategic use of the motor vehicle by rushing thousands of troops to the front in commandeered taxicabs and motorcars. For the most part, however, trucks were not used to transport troops, but rather to replace the mule- and horse-drawn escort wagon and supply train. The work performed here was prodigious. The maximum forward movement for a horse- or mule-drawn supply train was 10 to 15 miles a day; for a truck, 200, though an actual average of 50 miles a day was already a three-to-one advantage. Even more important than the greater speed were the flexibility of movement, the heavier loads, the inexhaustibility of power without the need for carrying provender.

The motorized supply train, however, had its own problems in moving on the unimproved wagon roads leading to the battlefields. Torrential rains buried the roads in axle-deep mud. The steady movement of artillery and ammunition trains, the marching troops, and the hoofs of cavalry had cut roadbeds into shreds. Nearer the front-line battlefields, roads dispersed into open fields, across the uneven terrain of ravines and gullies, up clay banks and rocky hillsides, where the heavy munition trucks slithered, mired, foundered, and, being dug out with shovel and pick and propped up with stone and planking, crawled relentlessly forward.

It was here that the Four Wheel Drive, with its turtlelike ability to extricate itself from the mud-choked mire and to pull itself forward with one wheel on a dry spot, demonstrated its inherent superiority. Sergeant W. J. Rickenbacker testified later to the truck's ability on the field of battle:

> I can only say, and will be backed up by some of the most eminent engineers of Europe and America, that it was one of the greatest factors in the defense of Verdun, Château-Thierry, and even Paris. The FWD's were found everywhere, hurrying supplies of all descriptions, where most needed, and at the right time, frequently turning the tide of battle, for without it our armies in the field would have been nothing for want of ammunition and supplies.

By the end of the war the United States government had shipped nearly 35,000 trucks to Europe, 24,000 of them engaged in supply and general cargo, 4,197 engaged in hauling ammunition, and another 5,000 in various other services, though this was conservatively estimated as less than 50 per cent of the number needed to supply two million men with the required 25,000 tons of daily supplies.

In addition to the transportation of supplies, the motor trucks were early used in a number of other ways, already indicating an on-the-battlefield adaptability characteristic of their later use on the farm, on the road, and in the field and factory. In the defense of Verdun they carried thousands of troops to the battlefield. On a number of occasions they were used in the transportation of light artillery. In moments of heavy battle losses, they served as improvised ambulances.

Writing a number of years later from a Canadian hospital, F. L. Crowhurst summed up the doughboy's point of view. Over with the 1st Canadian Battalion, he along with his company, mud-covered and exhausted, was resting by the roadside after a long march from below Vinny. Across the road in the open field, horse-drawn artillery was moving into position. One of the pieces was stuck in axle-deep mud, man and beast laboring to extricate the heavy wheels. Then a motor truck came down the road, swung off to the side, backed into position, hitched onto the gun, and with a slow, steady churning in the sticky clay pulled both itself and the gun from the mire.

"Some truck," said one of the men.

"An American FWD," said another.

"What does FWD stand for?" asked the first man.

"I don't know; maybe 'For Wonderful Delivery,'" said a third.

It was over a year later at the battle of Amiens, where he himself had been wounded, that the name came back to F. L. Crowhurst. Weary and exhausted from the long fighting and loss of blood, he stood by the roadside waiting for a lift back to the dressing station. It was only a mile or two, but that was a thousand more times than a fellow had strength to stumble, lifting his heavy feet and setting one foot ahead of the other. Then an empty supply truck came by and stopped for him. The driver helped him up, and he rode jolting and bouncing over the uneven road to the dressing station. It was after he had gotten down that he noticed the FWD. "For Wonderful Delivery," he thought to himself. Right or wrong, it would always be that to him.

On the morning of Armistice Day, November 11, 1918, the factory was still at the peak of its production. It was employing 1,600 men and producing trucks at the rate of twenty a day, or 600 a month. Rumors had been rife throughout the morning, and finally with the first ringing of church bells and the tooting of railroad whistles, pandemonium broke loose inside the factory as well. Some workers began to turn off machines, rushing up to congratulate each other; others began to cheer and shout above the din, still others grabbed flags and began a parade, the foremen giving way before the surging crowd, as a thousand men fell into step and marched through the factory to the office of W. A. Olen, who declared a public holiday on the spot. Marching out into the street, and led by the FWD band, they equipped themselves with cowbells, platters, horns, and circular saws and paraded until after midnight. They were celebrating not only the end of the war and the anticipated return of their sons and relatives, but also a job well done. They had built the trucks that had helped to turn the tide of battle. They had helped to transform the Four Wheel Drive Auto Company of Clintonville from the smallest to the largest four-wheel-drive factory in the world.

In 1911 the first factory building had provided floor space of 5,940 square feet. By 1918 the factory floor space utilized had risen to 185,351 square feet. In 1911 they had employed less than a dozen men on a payroll of $9,147.61; in 1918 the payroll had risen to $1,401,471.58. In 1911 they had built one car; in 1918 they were manufacturing at the rate of 10,000 trucks a year. In 1913 the assets of the company had been listed as $296,726; in 1918 they were $5,858,635. On an original capitalization of $110,000, later increased to $250,000, they had done a business of $27,000,000. In 1916 the capitalization of the company had been increased from $250,000 to $500,000 by a stock dividend of 100 per cent; in 1917 the capitalization had again been increased by a 100 per cent stock dividend to $1,000,000, and in 1918 to $1,500,000. In 1916 there had been a cash dividend of 15 per cent; in 1917 a cash dividend of 35 per cent; in 1918 a dividend of 14 per cent. Individual shares of stock had sold for $600 per share.

Back in 1912 two spinster sisters in Washington, D.C., largely at the suggestion of Captain Williams, had invested in 5 shares of Four Wheel Drive stock. For a number of years the investment had not looked promising. But by the end of 1918, on the initial investment of $500, they had received $1,290 in cash dividends; for the original 5 shares they now owned 30 shares, worth (at the current rate of $600 per share) $18,000.

Many another stockholder had profited likewise. If one adds the proportionate share of profits paid to the stockholders residing in Clintonville to the $2,500,000 paid out in wages to Clintonville workers in the period of eight years, one can see why the growing city began to count its needs. The war years had seen the building of 250 new homes, but there was still a need for 500 more. In 1917 they had built a new high school at a cost of more than $200,000, at that time rated as "the best high school building" in the state. What public-minded citizens now began asking for among themselves and in the pages of the *Tribune* were new improved and paved streets and roads, a city park, a new city hall, a library building, a municipal hospital, an up-to-date hotel, and a new city auditorium.

Clintonville was no longer in its own estimation merely a market center for a surrounding farming community; it was now an industrial center, primarily dependent upon a business in its midst which had in the current year done a gross of more than $19,000,000.

Among the citizenry, however, not all were equally happy. As in many other cases in American industrial history, the greatest reward did not go to the inventors. But as in many another case no one was really to blame. Back in 1910, at the time of the reorganization of the company, Otto Zachow and William Besserdich had been assigned 350 of the original 1,100 shares of stock in exchange for surrendering their basic patents to the company. At par value the stock then had a value of $35,000. In July of the next year, Otto, discouraged by the innumerable delays involved in manufacturing the first cars and unhappy with the internal bickerings in the company, petitioned the board of directors to buy his shares of stock. After some debate the board had agreed and purchased his holdings, 174 shares at the then market value of $57 per share, or a total of $9,000, and Otto went back to his machine shop on River Street, to the repair work on sawmills and threshing machines.

William Besserdich had held on to his shares somewhat longer. In 1913, however, no longer associated with his brother-in-law in the machine shop, he, too, had become discouraged and restless. He began selling his stock in small lots to B. A. Mosling and Charles Folkman, and in 1914 he petitioned the board to sell the remaining 91 shares to Charles Mahon. A disagreement over William's refusal to surrender the one patent taken out in his own name delayed the sale, but the company engineers rejecting the patent as insignificant, the sale was permitted. Before the year was out, the sale of trucks to the British having been made, Besserdich began to regret the move and for three years negotiated with the company in an effort to resell his patent. With that rejected he and Mosling withdrew and, moving to a neighboring city, began organizing a rival company for the manufacture of four-wheel-drive trucks.

There were others who had been disappointed. Back in 1912 and 1913 many a stockholder had relinquished the stock he had subscribed for, surrendering his down payment of 25 per cent, rather than sending good money after bad, as he thought, by paying up the remainder. Others whose stock had been paid for in cash, sold it again for whatever they could get, feeling it was better to realize a small return than to lose all. Now that one share had mushroomed into six and the cash dividends had more than paid for the stock, they became concerned with the rewards that had eluded them. Two years after the war, in 1920, five of them brought suit against Walter A. Olen and the board of directors, charging them with conspiracy to defraud the stockholders by concealment of the likelihood of British orders in the summer of 1914, a case fought through two courts, which both rendered in favor of the defendants.

For only one of the men associated with the company had the war years proved a spectacular bonanza. In 1912 P. J. F. Batenburg had arrived in America penniless. Later in that year he had gone to work for the company at a salary of $200 a month. In 1915 he had asked for a salary of $12,000 a year. The board of directors hesitated and then offered him $3,600 a year with a 1 per cent commission on sales. In the next three years he was to draw a commission of 1 per cent on $27,000,000 worth of business. Mr. Batenburg had rendered a distinguished service to the company both as superintendent and as chief engineer. His indefatigable energy, his engineering skill, his ability in factory organization had helped to design and to build 16,000 Model B trucks for the Allied governments. Unfortunately, a quarrel developed between Batenburg and the board of directors in 1918 over whether the commission should be paid before or after deduction for Federal taxes. Batenburg resigned from the company and brought suit in the Federal court at Milwaukee, which found in his favor against the company.

No one in 1914, of course, could have foreseen the prosperity ahead, no matter one's private dreams and hopes. Chance and fortune had played a role. Neither, for that matter, had anyone within the company made a private fortune or become one of the multimillionaires of the First World War era. The Four Wheel Drive Auto Company had been a *company* of manufacturers. Seven years earlier, at the time of the original organization, Walter A. Olen had made a public pronouncement that "no one individual was ever to grow up ahead of the company." What those in the company had realized in financial rewards, they had realized by working together, by sharing the hardships as well as the later successes.

From Chuckhole to Concrete

At a meeting in Chicago between truck manufacturers and officers from the War Department ten days before the signing of the Armistice, the future military needs of the United States Army were outlined as 50,000 trucks a year. Most of these were to be four-wheel-drive trucks, and the Army, having bought out the patent rights to the four-wheel-drive principle for $400,000, was now investigating the manufacturing facilities of some twenty plants, preparatory to letting new contracts. It looked then as if the Four Wheel Drive Auto Company would be taxed to its capacity for some time to come. Ten days later, with the war over, the need for 50,000 trucks had suddenly vanished in the surplus of some 30,000 needless trucks ready to be abandoned on the battlefields or in the military depots and arsenals of Europe and America. The disaster to the truck market was up to that time unparalleled in the annals of American industry. On one day the motor truck was a prized possession, essential to military victory, with every effort bent to secure its increased production; on the next it was a glut on the market, in many cases already an outmoded and obsolete vehicle.

During the war years there had been little time for basic redesign or truck engineering. Of the 16,000 trucks supplied by the Four Wheel Drive Auto Company, practically all of them had been the 3-ton Model B, a long, narrow truck, of cab-over-engine design, equipped with 42-inch wooden wheels and hard rubber tires, and powered by a four-cylinder, 36-horsepower motor. With its four-wheel-drive it had nevertheless proved to be the most singularly effective motor-driven vehicle in the First World War—its effectiveness being attested to not only in its selection by the British government for permanent display in the Crystal Palace War Exhibit, but also by its citation for distinguished service by the United States War Department and the inclusion of a scale model with its camouflaged ordnance body in the Smithsonian Institution.

But now that the war was over, there was a surplus even of Model B's. On the Continent more than 8,000 of them, shipped abroad for the military emergency, were sold by the United States to France and subsequently resold by the French government to private users. In England more than 3,000 of them were sold by the government to private concerns, which in turn went into the business of marketing trucks. In America, too, surplus trucks were auctioned off, sold to private dealers, and generally distributed throughout the country. Moreover, the United States government was distributing them under the recent highway-aid bills to the highway departments of the various states for road building and maintenance.

Concerned with war orders, the company had been forced

to neglect its commercial markets from 1916 to 1918. During the last year of the war, for instance, with U.S. government and foreign orders totaling nearly $19,000,000, its commercial sales had dropped to $251,747. Its experience with the Midwest Refining Company of Casper, Wyoming, had been typical. Three years earlier Midwest Refining had had a fleet of twenty-eight FWD's. Faced with the inability of the factory to furnish them with any more, or even to supply adequate spare and repair parts, the company had canceled future orders, traded off most of the FWD's, and refused at first even to allow the factory salesmen on the premises. At the end of the war the Four Wheel Drive Auto Company had one commercial representative abroad, Mr. C. S. Thomson, currently in South America. For a year or two the company could continue its manufacturing program, paying dividends to its stockholders from the surplus accumulated during the war years. That might give them time to reorganize and establish a domestic sales department, to reopen domestic markets, and to discover new ones. It would be the crucial test of the company's ability to survive.

The company met the crisis with confidence. In April of 1919 it organized a subsidiary factory at Kitchener, Ontario, and Joe Cotton, who since the beginning of the company had taken stock in lieu of cash for his advertising and had been elected to the board of directors the year before, left for Kitchener to become its first president. In the following year the company began negotiations with the Menominee Motor Truck Corporation, later buying it out, and moving the factory to Clintonville, a move designed to add a lighter 1-ton truck, the Hurryton, to its own line and to eliminate a rival concern. Branch offices were opened in

New York City, in Boston, Chicago, San Francisco, and Kansas City. At home the factory was reorganized into a modern industrial concern with its research, service, and safety departments; a modern metallurgical laboratory; a purchasing division; traffic, photographing, mailing, and inspection departments. The domestic sales department was reorganized into eight divisions covering the country, and a $100,000 advertising campaign was launched. By 1923 the foreign department had established seventy-three dealers in thirty-nine countries.

In spite of every effort, however, sales declined rather steadily up to 1925, or, perhaps more accurately, commercial sales did not materialize to offset the loss in government orders, which declined from 83 per cent of the total business in 1919 to 9 per cent in 1923 and then to nothing. From the beginning the Kitchener factory operated at a loss. Twenty per cent of all local dealers in motor trucks throughout the country failed in 1923. By 1924 most of the branch offices had been temporarily abandoned except for the New York one, operating at a loss. Employment had dropped from its high peak of more than 1,600 in 1918 to fewer than 500 men. The stock declined from its market value of $600 in 1918 to $90 per share, or $10 less than par value. In 1919 and 1920 cash dividends had continued to the stockholders, paid out of surplus profits of the war years. In 1921 and 1922 no dividends were issued and the annual operating loss had reached $69,383. In 1921, with Walter A. Olen, D. J. Rohrer, and Charles Folkman abroad to collect the final royalty payments from the English government, the stockholders had voted that the board of directors could close down the plant for an indefinite period. They were obviously anxious to conserve whatever profits they had made and ready to resist any expansion or even continued operation that might further deplete reserves. Many felt that with the overexpansion of the company, failure was imminent. Indeed, had the company failed, it would merely have suffered the fate of a majority of small companies in America. By 1924 seventy motor-truck companies had gone into the hands of receivers and into bankruptcy.

The most remarkable aspect of the history of the motor-truck industry is that it was exactly in the era of the twenties, when the sale of the motor truck had reached its lowest ebb, that the most spectacular and far-reaching developments took place. It was, for instance, exactly the period in which the motor truck itself helped to build and improve nearly a million miles of U.S. highways (which in itself made a new era of truck manufacturing possible by providing the highways for rapid and long-distance truck transportation), and it was also the era in which the truck exchanged its wagon-box hauling facilities for a far more specialized and adaptable service—on the highway, for the public utilities, in fire protection, and in oil-field operation.

The growth of the U.S. highway system itself is a part of the motor-truck story. Of the 2,151,379 miles of public roads in 1904, for instance, only 153,530 miles had been improved in any way, and none of them had been hard-surfaced. The first mile of concrete or hard-surfaced road had been laid in 1908 near Detroit. By 1914, the year the conflict broke out in Europe, 253,996 miles of road had been improved, and 3,296 miles had actually been hard-surfaced in concrete, brick, or stone block, but three thousand miles of hard surfacing in a road system of 2,500,000 miles was almost infinitesimal, and in the 250,000 miles of improved highways, little had been done to the dirt roads except to plow a drainage furrow alongside the roadbed or in some cases to cover the clay bed with a thin coat of gravel. The first real spurt in road building had come in 1916 with the Federal Aid Bill, which allocated some $75,000,000 a year of Federal funds, but little could be done during the war years. In 1921, however, when the Federal Highway Act of that year provided for an interstate highway system of Federal roads, "the most gigantic program of road building ever conceived" was launched. By 1924 Federal aid alone totaled $353,082,098, and the state and Federal aid combined reached the figure of $1,181,687,000. By that time 30,000 to 40,000 miles of roadway were being hard-surfaced a year, and half of the asphalt output of the country and 20 per cent of the concrete were going into highway construction. By the end of the decade, the total road system had increased to 3,000,000 miles, with more than 300,000 miles incorporated into Federal and state systems, and nearly one-third of the total, or 1,000,000 miles, had been improved, with nearly 200,000 miles of it hard-surfaced. (Ten years later the annual expenditure was to reach $1,000,000,000, and the Federal, state, and local governments would have hard-surfaced 1,000,000 miles of American roads.)

But that is the story told in statistics. To the average motorist and to the truck manufacturer it was a more graphic story told in terms of the roads he traveled, or in the case of the manufacturer, of the part his own trucks played in the transformation. Before 1914 few pleasure-car drivers, unless engaged in test runs or for experimental purposes, ever ventured far from home. A 50- to a 100-mile journey was a day's trip, in the course of which he might encounter a dozen different kinds of road conditions. Leading out from his own city would be two or three miles of hard-surfaced, narrow roadway, either of concrete or red brick. Later on, particularly in the summertime, the car might continue to spin on rather merrily over the hard-packed and even well-turned clay roadbed. In a dry season clouds of dust would envelop the vehicle and move along in its wake across the countryside. The clay road might give way to one of sand, slowing the forward movement to a crawl, or to a roadbed with a highly ridged center, the gravel scraping on oil pans and axles. A rainy season, or a sudden shower, would bring wagon-wheel ruts, strait-jacketing the steering wheels, or sticky, churning clay and bottomless sinkholes. A tire puncture or a faulty magneto might delay the long, laborious climb up the narrow roadway rounding to the top of a hill. In the end the driver might encounter another two or three miles of pavement leading into the town which had been his predetermined destination. Unless he was an extremely adventuresome soul, he did not dream of using his car for interstate transportation, and no one except for a few pioneering souls would have dreamed of a cross-continental tour.

By 1916, the latter, though extremely hazardous, was no longer an impossibility, and by 1920, a thousand tourists a summer were making the trip across the plains and the Rockies to the West Coast. Four years later, with the interstate highway system just beginning its development, a cross-continental traveler by railway train described the scene:

The car window panorama at every turn revealed motor tourists, both west bound and east bound, with their cars converted into veritable carryalls for human beings, baggage and camp equipment. From the vantage point I occupied, their trips across plains and deserts seemed everything I would want to avoid. Rough, unimproved roads, hot deserts, mud to contend with here and dust to battle against there . . . water to be carried for radiators perennially hot, vast stretches of burning sands to be crossed where life had been scorched and parched out of everything but the hardiest of desert flora and fauna.

Through the prairies of Indiana and Illinois and the rolling hills of Missouri ran the National Highway, one of the earliest of the transcontinental routes, a narrow lane between the tall rows of green corn, which obscured the intersecting rural highways and slowed traffic to a stop at every mile end; the roadway itself was a well-turned and well-dragged clay bed. Beyond the few miles of red-brick pavement leading out of Kansas City lay 700 miles of red-clay gumbo, which unseasonable rains turned into a mire.

All the way to the Colorado foothills of the Rockies, driving the road was a memorable adventure of mudhole and mire, of washed-out bridges, of missed detours around the stream-swollen arroyos, and later on of blistering sandstorms and of long-winding two-rutted lanes with sagebrush and cacti in the middle that led around the curving hills ever westward to the mountains. It was a lonely road, though already well traveled.

There were other roads leading across the prairies, like the Lincoln Highway and Pikes Peak Ocean to Ocean Highway, but whether one drove in Illinois, Iowa, Kansas, Oklahoma, or Texas, the red or black gumbo mudhole was always a present hazard. Typical of a thousand experiences is the following one of two young women, who on a Western trip were being eased out of a mudhole by two young farm hands.

The engine started, stalled, and started again a dozen times. At last the car stirred a bit from its lethargy, the two boys put their country strength against her broad back and pushed; the engine roared like a man-eating tiger—and we got out.

But we still had to conquer a black stretch of about a hundred yards, in which one of our rescuers had broken an axle, so he cheerfully told us, only yesterday. We were faced with the problem of to advance or to retreat. Either way was mud. We might get caught between two morasses, and starve to death before the sun dried the roads. We might turn back, but why return to conditions we had worked two hours to escape? We decided to advance. . . . "Race her for all she's worth," counseled the livelier of our rescuers, from the running board where he acted as pilot. I raced her . . . we wavered, struck a rut, and were gripped in it. . . . It led to a gruesome mass of black soup with a yawning hole at the bottom. "Here's where I broke my axle," shouted the pilot. To break the shock of dropping into the hole was to stick; to race ahead might mean a shattered car. There was no time to think it over. I pushed down on the gas. A fearful bump, and we went on, the mud sucking at the wheels every inch we advanced.

And after the mudholes and the mire there were long stretches of loose gravel and drifting sand.

Driving in those sandy tracks became a new sport. We learned to make the sand skid us around corners without decreasing our speed; we could calculate with nicety when a perceptible drag on the wheels warned us to shift gears. And they must be shifted instantly, for at a moment's delay the car sank deep, and the mischief was done which only shoveling could undo. Once we found ourselves facing another car blocking the road, sunk in the thick, unpacked sand. We could not turn out, and an instant's stop put us in a like predicament. They wistfully asked us to pull them out, but as we were heavier than they, and would have made two obstacles instead of one in the road, we had to refuse the only help asked of us, who had so many times been the beneficiaries. We left them to an approaching mule team, after they had returned good for evil and pushed us out.

And after the plains came the foothills, with the road winding ever upward, and finally the sheer wall of the Rockies, with the canyons opening inward and upward, the narrow gravel road hanging onto the side of the cliff.

Far below the river was a tiny thread, getting tinier every moment. On the very edge of the fast deepening canyon hung the road, with neither fence nor wall. . . . As we climbed, the road narrowed till for a dozen miles no car could have passed us. Regularly it twisted in such hairpin curves that our front tires pinched our back tires as we made the turn. Instead of being graded level, the road rose and fell so steeply in rounding curves that the car's hood completely concealed which way the road twisted. . . . If we went left while the road turned right, we should collide with the cliff; if the road turned left and we right, we should be plunged into space. . . . At that giddy moment, on the very highest spot, I essayed to turn a sharp corner down grade, where a ledge threw us well over to the edge of the curve, and I found my foot brake would not hold. I tried the emergency. It too, had given way from the constant strain put on it. The road ahead switchbacked down, down, down. . . . Deciding something had to be done quickly, I ran the "Old Lady's" nose into the ledge. The left fender bent in towards the engine, but we stuck.

The point of all this is, of course, not the roads themselves nor the story of a transcontinental tour. By 1924 the annual car registration had reached the phenomenal figure of more than 13,000,000 and by the end of the decade, in 1930, an interstate highway system of improved and graveled roads stretched from the Mississippi to the Golden Gate. Two decades later, by 1950, all America lay crisscrossed by over 1,500,000 miles of concrete and asphalt, double and four-lane highways, overheads and underpasses, banked curves and easy gradients, leading from city to city, from farmland to market, through the mountain passes to the ocean, able to accommodate the nearly 40,000,000 automobiles and the nearly 5,000,000 motor trucks now engaged in long- and short-distance transportation. And this miracle of transformation owed itself primarily, at least in its initial stages, to the motor truck.

It was the motor trucks of the twenties, the Model B's equipped with dump-truck bodies, whether Whites or Packards or Pierce-Arrows or Jefferys or the Nash Quads or the FWD's, that had helped to scoop out and haul away the mountainsides and fill up the valleys, bank the curves and build up the overpasses, dumping billions and billions of tons of dirt and boulders into place, hauling billions of tons of concrete and gravel, and after the roads were built assisted in maintaining them for service, keeping the mountain passes and the roads of the plains free from snow and ice, rebuilding and reconditioning the feeder roads with drag and scraper. By 1924 the United States government had given more than 30,000 surplus trucks to the various state highway departments for road-building and maintaining purposes. The majority of them had been FWD's. By 1924, for instance, West Virginia had 289 FWD trucks, North Carolina 300, Iowa 300, Nebraska 160, and Colorado 325— some of them still in use today after more than thirty years of service.

Back in 1923 Walter A. Olen had been right in reporting to the stockholders that the Federal gift of trucks to the state highway departments was hurting the truck business, and the sale of surplus war trucks and trainloads of spare parts was crippling and destroying new markets, but fortunately he and the board of directors had adopted a far-seeing policy. "Let us not lament the gift of the Federal trucks," Mr. Olen said. "In the long run they will build us new markets. Let us concentrate now on servicing the trucks, on supplying the highway departments with spare parts, and seeing that our trucks are doing the jobs assigned them."

To implement the policy, the Four Wheel Drive Auto Company built up its service department, sending out twenty to thirty men a year to visit the state highway departments, to train the drivers and mechanics in the use and servicing of the trucks. Early in the twenties the sale of spare parts had risen to nearly a million dollars per year. But more important than the sale of spare parts was the good will won and maintained, the increased efficiency of the operating trucks, and the engineering skills and knowledge and field experience of the state engineers, which was exchanged with the factory representatives and so brought to bear upon new designs and developments. Between 1923 and 1928 the old Model B was completely redesigned and rebuilt until nothing was left of the original truck except the clutch, the ball and socket, and the universal joint, and in later years many of the new and more powerful models owed their new compression ratio or a new design in the differential or chassis structure to the experience of the state engineers in the field. In one sense at least the later FWD's were and are today trucks designed in the field and under operating conditions, tested and built to meet the needs of the operators.

Even without the testimony of the men in the field who operated, drove, and repaired the early Model B's, men like Walter Root and Charles Kinderman of the Iowa State Highway Department, or Fred Putney of Nebraska, or Richard Carlson and Fritz Altwater of the Liberty Truck and Parts Company in Denver, or Russell Stalnaker of the California Highway Department, it would be easy to see the role of the FWD in the highway program. Equipped to drive on all four wheels, to plow through and over and into a terrain unmanageable for rear-drives alone, able to ascend grades up to 70 per cent, to lift themselves like a land turtle across furrows and over boulders one wheel at a time, sturdy enough to stand the impact of the daily wear and tear and the thud of a ton scoop of dirt and boulders released from the iron-clawed steam shovel, the FWD's bore the bulk of the labor. "You couldn't wear them out, and you couldn't tear them apart," Kinderman said many years later. "It took a two hundred pound man to steer them and the ride was like that of a rough, bucking bronco, but they burrowed down and pulled like six yoke of oxen, and you could never tire the damn things out."

"I serviced hundreds of them in France, before I came back to Central City and later down here to Denver, where Fritz Altwater and I organized the Liberty Truck and Parts Company to service the state highway trucks, and later took over the agency for FWD's and sold hundreds more," said Dick Carlson, who has seen the state highway system of Colorado grow from 10 miles of improved roads in 1919 to a state system of 12,400 miles, nearly half of it hard-surfaced and containing 75 per cent of all the roads of the nation at an elevation of 10,000 feet or higher. "In my experience," said Russell Stalnaker of the California State Highway Department, now retired, "no single piece of equipment played a more important role in the development and maintenance of the California State Highway System than the motor truck. And among the motor trucks, none of them was comparable to the FWD."

Open Roads for Winter Driving CHAPTER SEVEN

The second spectacular development that came after the First World War, in the era of the twenties, at the very time the truck market itself had seemed to reach its nadir, was the continuing evolutionary specialization and adaptation of the motor truck itself. Before the war and during it, and even as late as the early twenties, the essential characteristic of the motor truck was that of a self-propelled wagon. Its chief use lay in hauling, and its primary adaptation to working conditions was the choice between the platform, open or railed, and the wagon-box or carryall construction. Of 400,000 motor trucks then in use, four-fifths were of the simple 1-ton variety and basically still consisted of modifications of passenger-car chassis to make them more adaptable to the transportation of merchandise. The only recognizable division then in the trucking industry was that between a light-duty and a heavy-duty truck.

By 1930 a truck was no longer merely a truck, and a term such as "a standard truck" was inapplicable. To be sure, the essential parts were still there—the engine, the wheels, a mechanism to carry the power from the engine to the wheels, brakes, a steering gear, and a structure with which to tie the units together and in or upon which to transport something—but beyond that the earlier and later truck had little resemblance. The earlier trucks were single-purpose vehicles limited in their adaptations. The later trucks were multiple-purpose vehicles, highly specialized and adapted to perform specific functions under operating conditions which varied almost as much as the jobs they were called upon to perform. They were ready now for both on-the-highway and off-the-road service. They could carry 1 ton or 25. In highway work they scraped, pushed, and dragged. They were able to pull ten times their own weight in trailers and semitrailers. They had been adapted to carry liquids, like gasoline and milk; materials as fragile as eggs and china, as crude as coal and cement blocks, as diverse as cabbages and dynamite or household furniture and kitchen garbage; and they were equally well adapted for a high-speed transcontinental run or a house-to-house delivery. No invention in the industrial field had adapted itself to more uses, become more specialized in terms of its operating conditions, or more drastically transformed the economy and the standard of living of the American people. The development was steady and, at least at first, more concerned with basic engineering than spectacular performance.

Central, of course, to the development of the truck was the engine power. The earlier Model B had been powered with a four-cylinder gasoline engine developing 30 to 40 horsepower and capable of a speed up to 20 and 30 miles per hour. The introduction and designing of completely new engines in the early twenties, and the introduction of the six-cylinder motor and later diesels, gave rise to engines capable of 110 horsepower and later to horsepowers of 200 and over, with a maximum-efficiency speed of 60 and 70 miles per hour. The old engines had been built for a first life of 20,000 to 30,000 miles before major overhauling and repair; the later engines had a first life of 75,000 to 100,000 miles, and many a truck by 1930 had passed the million-mile mark, and 400,000 to 500,000 miles were considered easy. All this had been accomplished, too, with a reduction in actual engine weight and as much as a 20 per cent reduction in fuel and operating costs. Twenty years earlier it had taken 6 quarts of lubricating oil for every 100 gallons of gasoline, and in later engines this had been reduced to 1 quart. For every dime the later operator spent on service, the earlier operator had had to spend one dollar.

With the increase in horsepower came other changes. The earlier truck had been equipped with three standard speeds, which permitted the driver, in starting the vehicle or in pulling heavy loads or in climbing grades, to select one of three ratios in the gears which transmitted power from the engine to the wheels. This limited both the pulling power of the truck and the efficiency of operation. A high ratio stalled the engine when the pull was heavy; a low ratio consumed needless fuel where the going was easy. The early Model B, for instance, had had a ratio in low gear of 48 to 1, the maximum permissible in terms of the materials and the structure of the truck itself. In 1926 the Four Wheel Drive Auto Company bought the manufacturing rights to the Cotta transmission and redesigned it, to give later trucks a gear ratio as low as 140 to 1. Flexibility had been increased to five speeds forward, and later, as the range between pulling power and high-speed operation on the highway became greater, ten and twelve speeds forward, with auxiliary transmissions providing a reduction of ratio as low as 600 to 1 for a heavy pull. In the late thirties, double reduction axles and later multiple-speed axles had been added, providing for greater and greater flexibility, efficiency in operation, and ease in handling.

Similar improvements took place in the clutches, for with the multiple speeds ease in shifting was essential; in doubling and tripling the strength of the axles, thus increasing the carrying load and the pulling power; in increasing the braking power by braking on all four wheels, for increased safety and ease of operation; by the development of a more effective and easier steering mechanism; and in providing ever larger and longer and more effective springs to reduce the shock on the other parts of the truck and so ensure longer over-all durability.

Certainly one of the largest single factors in the development of the later motor truck, particularly in the commercial-transportation field, was the development of the steel wheel and the pneumatic tire. The earlier trucks, and all heavy-duty trucks well into the late twenties, had been equipped with wooden wheels and solid rubber tires, which limited the speed of the vehicle with their low tractional ability and their low resilience to road shock. With the introduction of the steel wheel and the pneumatic tire came increased speeds, infinitely greater traction and pulling power, and a reduction of the wear and tear from road shock and vibration on the moving vehicle. Even the earlier pneumatic tires had required an air pressure of 60 pounds on a 4-inch tire, so that the speed and the carrying power were still limited; but in the later twenties with the development of the low-pressure balloon tire, even the heaviest-duty trucks could be equipped with pneumatics. This not only enormously increased their carrying and pulling power, the speed of operation, and the road ease (the last of which permitted the transportation of such breakable goods as eggs and glassware), but with the increased traction permitted dozens of adaptations for the motor truck hitherto impossible.

A second factor of equal significance in the development of the truck was the increased knowledge of metallurgy. Here the Four Wheel Drive Auto Company, by a happy chance, again became one of the leaders in the development. James Sorenson was a well-trained metallurgist and engineer who during the First World War was engaged in testing cannon forgings for the Ordnance Department of the U.S. Army. Early in 1918 he had run an advertisement in a metallurgical publication offering his services. One of the three replies he had received came from Walter A. Olen. Neglecting to look up Clintonville on the map, he bought a ticket on the Northwestern Railroad, thinking the village was probably somewhere near Milwaukee. Surprised at the price of the ticket, he asked the distance. "You're bound for the blueberry bogs of northern Wisconsin," the agent replied.

Sorenson arrived at the Clintonville station at one in the morning, rode the Ward House bus through the deserted streets, and accepted the only room available—a small, dingy, and infrequently used one in the hotel. In the morning his one concern was to return to Chicago as speedily as possible, but finding that the next train did not leave until two o'clock in the afternoon, he decided to pass the time by at least looking at the factory he had come to see. There he met W. A. Olen, P. J. F. Batenburg, and Harry Dodge, the engineer. Before the afternoon train arrived, he had decided to throw in his lot with the new company.

Of primary importance in the building of a more powerful truck was the strength of the materials—the tensional strength of the structural steel, the torsional strength of the axle and propeller shafts, and the hardness and durability of the gears. All this in turn depended upon the selection of alloys, upon the forgings and stampings, and upon the heat-treatment of the steel and its proper quenching. The basic concern was always for increasing the strength and durability without increasing the weight of the material. Under Sorenson's skillful management, gear steels giving greater strength and longer fatigue life were selected, and the gear-cutting machinery was modified to permit shaving gears to an almost infinitesimal accuracy under an oil-quenching method that reduced or eliminated the earlier heat distortion. Through this improvement, gears capable of transmitting the 200 horsepower of the engine to the pulling and driving wheels were produced. The torsional strength of the axles was doubled and tripled without any increase in weight. Propeller shafts were developed from selected steel alloys that with scientifically controlled heat-treatment produced four times the torsional strength of earlier shafts, with at the same time a 50 per cent reduction in weight.

Within a few years the Four Wheel Drive Auto Company had become one of the leaders in building heavy-duty trucks capable of hauling 5- and 10-ton loads. They had been among the first to introduce the use of vanadium steels, which gave greater strength and elasticity to gears, springs, frames, and axles. From the very beginning the Four Wheel Drive truck had made use of a center differential that allowed for a flexible flow of power to the driving wheels. The company had been the first to substitute the sturdier steel wheel for the earlier wooden-spoke and center-hub construction.

But all of these were improvements in truck engineering, taking place for the most part within the factory walls and so to the layman less spectacular than the external adjustments and adaptations of the motor truck to a particular job —though it was primarily the increase in power and durability that permitted the adaptations. In the building of the highways, for instance, the earlier Model B's had been engaged primarily in moving supplies and in hauling dirt fill and gravel, where the extra four-wheel traction enabled the Model B's to get in and out of gravel pits and through the soft materials of the construction site with greater ease than other vehicles could. Of equal importance, however, to the U.S. highway system, whether Federal, state, or local, once the road was built, was the maintenance of a roadbed, particularly of the thousands of miles of improved and graveled roads. In the early history of road building, maintenance was almost entirely dependent upon horse-drawn drags and scrapers, but with the engineering of a more powerful heavy-duty motor truck came the development of the motor-truck scraper, front mounting, or underbody blade, that could do the work of ten and twenty horse-drawn rigs. Ridges and ruts could now be plowed out, the side-thrown gravel returned to the roadbed, the corrugated, washboard ridges smoothed off and filled, all in one operation with a truck moving along at 15 to 20 miles per hour.

It is well to remember that many of the early roads, even when improved and graveled, were apt to be no more than narrow lanes, allowing for the usual wagon-wheel tread of 56 inches, the common tread of the early truck and motorcar as well. As the motor traffic itself increased and the engineers lowered and widened the design of the automobile and motor truck and thus increased the width of the wheel tread, thousands upon thousands of miles of improved roads had to be rebuilt once more, the roadbed widened, the ditches alongside filled, and a 6-foot berm built up. It was in the rebuilding of the roads, in the widening and maintaining of the roadbed against the steadily increasing stream of traffic, the wear and tear of a million wheels on clay or gravel in a dry summer or a wet spring or the freezing and thawing of fall and winter, that the motor-truck scraper came fully into its own.

Almost simultaneously with the ever-increasing highway system and the rebuilding and widening of roads came the demand for the all-year road and the necessity for snow and ice removal. The earlier motorcar and even the truck were primarily summertime vehicles; hence the design of the early touring car and the open-air cab. With the increased dependence upon motor transportation and the steady improvement of the highway, people in the Middle and Northern states were no longer content with summertime driving, no longer willing to resort during the months of ice and snow to horse-drawn vehicles and bobsleds. From the motor-truck scraper to the snowplow was but a single step, and within a few years the motor truck had once again revolutionized the traffic and transportation habits of more than half of the country. No longer was it necessary during the winter months to store the automobile or the motor truck in a garage, emptying the radiators, jacking up the wheels, and removing the tires. No longer was the open-air touring car a satisfactory design. With winter driving came the enclosed sedan, the closed cab on a truck, windshield wipers, and heating units, all making for summerlike comfort, though not without increasing the traffic hazards. Within a decade, from 1920 to 1930, the motor-truck snowplow had practically equalized summer and winter traffic, whether in a thousand normally snowbound Northern communities or on the transcontinental highways crossing the Great Plains or climbing through the passes in the high Rockies.

To meet the needs of highway maintenance and winter driving, the Four Wheel Drive Auto Company had early begun experimenting with the motor-truck scraper and snowplow. The first motorized V-type snowplow in the country, built of planks and scrap iron, was mounted on a Model B by Schemerhorn and Wright of Granville, New York, in 1920. During the same year the Tomahawk Pulp and Paper Company of Tomahawk, Wisconsin, began experimenting with a straight-blade plow made from an old boiler plate, again mounted on a Model B. This proved more satisfactory, though there were still engineering difficulties involved. Up until that time few trucks had been built that could stand the repeated impact of a power-driven plow encountering the well-packed and incrusted snowdrifts of the open road or mountain passes. To engineer the project, the Four Wheel

Drive Auto Company set up a clay-bank test, repeatedly driving a truck equipped with a snowplow, head on, under full power, into a bank of red clay at speeds up to 25 miles per hour. In the early tests the snowplows broke, the mountings gave way, axle shafts twisted off, springs broke, and the frame of the truck itself twisted. But out of the experiment and the work of the metallurgists and engineers came a truck that revolutionized road maintenance and snow removal, an FWD that could bear the impact of the clay bank thousands of times without damage to truck or plow. Within a few years the company had evolved a single-unit road maintainer for hauling, grading, road repair, and snow removal, performing at speeds up to 30 miles per hour, equipped with an underbody blade scraper and able to mount a gigantic V- or side-blade snowplow, the entire rig capable of withstanding pressures up to 9,000 pounds.

By 1930 motor trucks were maintaining a million miles of improved highways and keeping them open for winter driving. The second decade, 1930 to 1940, saw a further development in the snowplow from the V- and single-blade type, to the gigantic V with side wings, the auger plow, and the rotary, capable of throwing snow 150 feet to the side of the road at the rate of 60 tons per minute, with a comparable increase in motor-truck power and in the variety of trucks available, from the light 3-ton trucks to the giant diesels of 25-ton capacity and 200 horsepower.

Throughout the development, the Four Wheel Drive, because of its greater traction and sturdy construction, remained a favorite of the highway departments, both state and local. By 1940 more than 8,000 of them were operating on the highways of America. At the end of still another decade, in 1950, the FWD was in service for snow removal in every state within the snow belt, in every province of Canada. The State of New York alone had more than a thousand Four Wheel Drive trucks in operation; Pennsylvania had 350, including a fleet of specialized crash trucks and seventeen snowplows for the famous Pennsylvania Turnpike; Colorado had 163; California, 158. The same Four Wheel Drive trucks were operating in far-off Hammerfest, the northernmost city in the world; in the Alps of central Europe; in Korea; in India and Pakistan; in Egypt and Africa; in the high Andes and Tierra del Fuego, in Magallanes, the southernmost city in the world. Not only on American highways but on highways all over the world the FWD's from Clintonville were building and maintaining roads and keeping them open for winter driving.

More graphic than statistics to the citizens of Clintonville and stockholders in the company were stories of the truck's performance—stories of records broken, of new highways traversed, of roads opened, and of rescues made.

In 1940 and again in 1941 an FWD won the snow fighter's rodeo sponsored by the Michigan State Highway Department in cooperation with the Michigan College of Mining and Technology and the Upper Peninsula Road Builders' Association, held at Isle Royale Sands near Houghton, where among twelve competing teams of drivers and trucks, the FWD, driven by Rudolph Putansu and Clarence Benson, plowman, cleared 500 feet of road, 20 feet wide, in the record time of 5 minutes and 30 seconds. The second truck, a conventional rear-drive, had taken 18 minutes.

In 1947 an FWD made the first winter trip by motor truck from Sheridan on the National Railway to the village of

Pukitawogan on the north shore of Hudson Bay, a 139-mile run over old lumber trails, leading across frozen lakes and over corduroy bridges, through 2 to 3 feet of packed snow at 25 degrees below zero, to bring supplies to a trading post. During the same winter another truck broke a 32-mile blockade from Ferndale Corners to Tobermory at the end of Bruce Peninsula, through 15-foot drifts, in order to bring relief to marooned families and an expectant mother.

In 1950 the Laramie River road in the northern Colorado Rockies lay blocked with 210 inches of snow that had fallen between Christmas Day and January 22, as blizzard after blizzard raced across the heights, one storm alone having added 69 inches. Forty ranchers in the mountains were cut off from the outside world and supplies were getting low. The Laramie County Highway Department had been trying to open the road but had found it impossible to buck the 8- and 10-foot drifts, packed so solidly that horsemen could ride over them without difficulty. Army officials had tried to bring in some rotary plows from Lowry Field near Denver, but there had been unfortunate delays. Finally the state highway department called the Liberty Truck and Parts Company of Denver. A big Model M7 FWD had arrived a few days earlier and was being demonstrated by Dick Carlson and A. M. Dahm near Fort Collins. Receiving the call, the men drove back to Laramie and then south on the Laramie River road, where, after returning to Denver for heavy clothes, sleeping bags, and emergency rations, they were ready for the assigned task. Starting up the river road the next morning, they hit 5- and 6-foot drifts of solidly packed snow on an 8 per cent grade. The chunks broke off in blocks weighing 2 and 3 tons. "You'll never make it," an old rancher said. "This is the worst winter since 1888." At the end of the first day they had made 5 miles. The next morning, in below-zero weather, the plowing continued. Sometimes the big truck could make only 6 feet, hitting a bank of 10-foot snow at 25 miles per hour. In the end they plowed out 27 miles of road, climbing and winding upward from 7,000 feet to an elevation of 8,300 feet, and with the main road open were ready to attack the branch roads and spurs.

During the winter of 1952 the greatest snowstorm in fifty years swept over northern California, burying roads and blocking traffic. In the high Sierras 8 feet of snow and more fell in one week; in the Donner Pass area, on U.S. Highway 40, the fall was 138 inches, making a total since early in December of more than 200 inches of snow. Howling winds at velocities of 75 to 100 miles per hour drove the freshly fallen snow into mountainous drifts, isolating communities, starting dangerous avalanches, and halting traffic. On January 14 the *City of San Francisco*, a crack streamliner on the Southern Pacific, was stalled near Yuba Gap with 256 passengers aboard.

From the first day of the storm every man and piece of equipment in the California Highway Department had been hard at work. Huge push plows and rotaries had been brought from as far away as Los Angeles and Hollywood. Battling the mountainous drifts, the dump trucks, equipped with 10-foot concave blades, their truck beds filled with sand and gravel for added weight, were unequal to the task. Only the huge rotaries, with their 6-foot augers and the whirling fan of the powerful blower spewing aside a 100-foot stream of white snow, could eat their way through. At Twin Bridges a huge snowslide had covered the store and resort building, killing two occupants. Another avalanche had carried a huge snowplow off the highway and 300 feet down a precipitous slope. A similar slide on U.S. Highway 50 had swept a giant radio-equipped rotary off the roadbed, turned it over, and buried it under 5 feet of snow. The driver, calling for help, had later managed to dig his way to the surface, though rescuers who had rushed to the scene had spent over an hour finding two workmen, only one of whom survived.

On the day the *City of San Francisco* became marooned near Yuba Gap, one of the rotaries on U.S. 40 was working at Baxters, 10 miles to the east, cut off by 25-foot drifts. A second rotary, 6 miles away, was digging out and rescuing two snowbound push plows. With the trucks freed, the caravan turned back toward Yuba Gap. After a mile or so the windshield wiper on the rotary broke in the whirling, freezing snow, and the truck, moving blindly, had run over a bank. Without the rotary the other trucks were helpless, and the men, abandoning the trucks for the night, fought their way through the howling darkness to a small lodge near Butts Lake, where they first heard of the streamliner's plight. Returning to the trucks in the morning, they cleared the roadway with shovels and got the rotary back onto the road by four in the afternoon. By four o'clock the next morning they had plowed their way to Yuba Gap; and, a new crew taking over, the giant rotary gouged out a narrow lane to the stranded train, permitting the passengers to be transferred to a relief train at Nyack. Before the storm was over,

400 motor-truck plows and more than 1,200 men had engaged in the battle.

The Four Wheel Drives had not only played a major role in building the roads; now with ten times the power and ever-increasing sturdiness they were ready to maintain them and keep them open.

Across the Mountains, in the   CHAPTER
Cities, and Deep into the Earth   EIGHT

Paralleling the adaptation of the motor truck to the building and maintaining of our highways was its adjustment to the more specialized needs of public utilities, of fire protection, and of oil-field operations. Engaged in work less obvious to the public, the motor truck has in such areas played a role equally central in the development of American economy and the establishment of our current habits and ways of life. Many times the industry and the motor truck have advanced together, the industry dependent upon the motor truck and the motor truck reaching new developments as it sought to meet the industry's needs. In the field of public utilities, for instance, the increase of hydroelectric power, the construction of transmission lines, rural electrification, the stringing of millions of miles of telephone wire were possible only because the motor truck increasingly became a specialized and highly effective unit.

Before the development of the motor truck nearly all the work had to be manual or powered by horses. The pick and shovel and mule- and horse-drawn scrapers and wagons had built the dams and the sluiceways; horse-drawn wagons had hauled the supplies for the power stations and transported the 30- to 70-foot poles to location for the stringing of the wires. Manual labor had dug the holes, thirty to forty per mile, 16 to 36 inches in diameter, 5 to 8 feet deep, in sand or clay or mountain shale and boulder. Then a crew of five or six men with their pickpoles or rope and tackle had raised the pole upright and lowered it into position, ready for the wire. With the arrival of the earlier motor truck it had been possible to transport men and materials to location, and even to haul the poles themselves, but without facilitating or speeding up the basic operation.

By 1916 a motor-driven earth borer or auger for digging holes had been mounted onto horse-drawn wagons, and gasoline engines were doing some of the digging in the easier soil formations. Any further assistance, however, awaited the development of the heavy-duty truck, equipped with a power take-off for the earth borer and the tractional ability to negotiate the rugged terrain of this off-the-road service. In 1923, through negotiations with the American Telephone and Telegraph Company, the Four Wheel Drive Auto Company secured the rights to the International earth-boring machine and began mounting it onto Model B trucks. Similar experiments were going on elsewhere, and within a year or two, with the development of the more powerful engine and the sturdier frames necessary for the rugged work, the motor truck, equipped with the earth borer and an integral derrick and winch to raise the poles and lower them into the hole, had revolutionized the telephone and power-transmission industry. By 1926 the Postal Telegraph Company of New York, in building a line from Fort Worth, Texas, to Los Angeles, a distance of 1,550 miles, using the earth borer, dug holes and set poles at a rate of nearly 100 a day and completed during the period from January to September a project for which the original contract had allotted two years. By 1927, fifty-three public-utility companies were using the new equipment of the Four Wheel Drive Auto Company.

With the arrival of new motorized equipment, the growth in electric power and transmission lines in the twenties and thirties was spectacular. Within a decade thousands of new streams had been harnessed with dams and sluiceways and penstocks; a hundred thousand turbines had begun supplying consumers with electric power earlier undreamed of. Thousands of steam-generating plants, augmenting hydroelectric power, had begun to dot the countryside. In the decade from 1920 to 1930, for instance, the capacity of the electric generating plants throughout the country grew from 12,000,000 to 33,000,000 kilowatts. In the next decade it increased to 40,000,000 and within another leaped forward to 62,000,000. The electrification of rural areas increased from 190,000 farms in 1925 to 4,500,000 by 1948. Every kilowatt produced by the generators and every farm electrified added to the total number of poles and the endless miles of wire.

In 1900 a transmission line 20 miles long, capable of carrying 3,000 horsepower of electric energy at 11,000 volts, had been an extraordinary engineering feat. In 1928 lines were being built capable of delivering 125,000 horsepower a distance of 250 miles over a single circuit at 22,000 volts. By 1950 high-power transmission lines built and manned by motor truck stretched from the Atlantic Seaboard to the Pacific, reaching from city to city, across the plains and high over the mountains, spanning broad valleys and a thousand miles of desert, linking system to system, covering the entire country with a network of steel and wire from Portland, Maine, to San Diego, California.

In the high Sierras, from more than a hundred private lakes and reservoirs lost among snow-covered mountain tops, through a thousand miles of canals and tunnels, one company alone by 1950 was delivering nearly 4,000,000 horsepower of electric energy to more than 2,000,000 consumers in an 89,000-square-mile area, with a network of lines capable of thrice encircling the earth. To patrol its lines and power stations, day and night, in bad weather and good, at the source of its energy and to the door of the consumer, the company manned a fleet of more than 4,000 cars and trucks. Many of them—and always, when a heavy-duty truck was in demand—were FWD's.

A strikingly similar development had taken place in the telephone and telegraph industry. In 1920 there were some 13,000,000 telephones, comprising a system of poles and wires and underground cables stretching to 32,000,000 miles. By 1930 the number of telephones had risen to 20,000,000 and the length of wire to 83,000,000 miles. In 1950 the number of telephones had doubled to more than 44,000,000, and the miles of poles and wire reached the figure of 150,000,000.

The building and maintenance of these millions of miles of telephone and telegraph and high-power-transmission lines demanded increasing power and flexibility in the motor truck, from lighter 3-ton units, able to dig holes up to 20 inches in diameter, to the giant 12-ton trucks, capable of digging holes 14 feet deep and up to 54 inches in diameter. The work demanded a truck for all sorts of terrain, capable of operating on the level road, in the ditches along the highway, in the open field, across bog and mire, up the steep mountainside, over boulder and cliff no highway ascends. It was here that the four-wheel-drive principle proved indispensable and the foresight of the Four Wheel Drive Auto Company was demonstrated. By 1930 the factory had trucks operating in the utility field in every state of the Union; it had shipped trucks to Europe and far-off Australia. By 1940 it had developed highly specialized maintenance units for all kinds of operating conditions: trucks equipped with earth borers, pole-setting derricks, power winches, linesmen's tools, a six-man full-crew cab for transportation to and from location (eliminating the need for separate conveyance, or for riding in the open body of the truck with exposure to the weather or the danger of falling tools and equipment). It had demonstrated its ability to go anywhere at any time to meet the needs of flowing power.

In February, 1938, a cloudburst broke over the Los Angeles area. Rains fell steadily from Saturday evening through Sunday and Monday and well into the next week. Twenty miles from the city the 110,000-volt, steel-tower transmission line of the Los Angeles Bureau of Power and Light crossed the big Tujunga Wash. By Wednesday, 25 inches of rain had fallen, and the normally dry bed of the wash was a raging torrent nearly a mile wide. Bridges, railway tracks, highways, and houses had been swept away. Two of the huge tower footings had given way and the lines lay sagging and broken. The city of Los Angeles was in darkness. Late on Wednesday, two linesmen, driving an FWD weighted down with a 4-ton concrete slab for ballast, attempted a trial run to the towers through the 4 feet of swiftly churning water, over hidden boulders, fallen trees, sandbanks, washouts, and debris. It was an act of desperation, the men fully expecting that they might be stalled or that the truck might even turn over. Plunging in and over, turning this way and that in the whirling waters to avoid floating debris, dropping into washouts and crawling over sand ridges, the truck made the run and thereafter, for a period of 48 hours, made trip after trip, hauling men and materials to the work of restoring the flow of power.

"It's like a gray goose," said one of the drivers. "It waddles and swims and does damn near anything but fly."

Back in 1917 the Four Wheel Drive Auto Company had built its first fire truck and sold it to the city of Minneapolis. Designed to replace the horse-drawn steam-engine pumper, the new truck had quickly enough demonstrated its superiority in the speed with which it moved through muddy, unpaved streets of the city. With four-wheel traction it could swing around corners with the ease of a horse-drawn vehicle or back its way to an open stream from which to pump water. With the pumper, driven by the truck motor, it needed no separate fire kindled on the way, and there were no delays while waiting for steam. Within two years the company had sold seven more to Minneapolis, and the next year they had built one for the city of Clintonville.

Then the war years had intervened, and the entire product of the factory had gone into Model B's for the European battlefield. With the war over, the company had returned to the concern with domestic markets and in 1923 turned once more to the building of fire trucks. That very year, the older truck built for the city of Clintonville helped to save the neighboring city of New London from what threatened to be a very destructive fire.

At noon on January 1, when the fire broke out and a frantic call went out to surrounding cities for help, a heavy snow with drifts 2 and 3 feet deep covered the 16 miles of road between New London and Clintonville. A dozen business houses on the main street were already on fire, so the call reported, and the entire business district was likely to go up in flames. New London's fire-fighting equipment at the time was an old 350-gallon steam pumper and a 1½-ton truck equipped with a small chemical tank.

The call had come to Clintonville shortly before one o'clock. By two o'clock the Clintonville truck had battled the 16 miles through the drifts and over the slippery roads and was pumping two streams of water, at the rate of 600 gallons a minute, onto the burning buildings. For 7 hours, from two in the afternoon until nine at night, the pumping continued, but in the end the fire had been put out and the greater portion of the city had been saved. A truck from the neighboring city of Appleton, equally far distant, had not arrived until nearly six in the evening. The next week a re-organized fire department of New London came to Clinton-ville to buy a new truck.

Later on in the same year a fire broke out at Neopit, en-veloping a huge sawmill and lumberyard. With a strong northwest wind fanning the flames, the piled lumber and the heavy timber roared skyward. The entire village with the homes of 300 workers was in danger. Calls for help had gone out to Antigo, Gillett, Shawano, and Clintonville.

Workers themselves were fighting the flames with whatever seemed available, buckets of water dipped from the stream or filled at nearby pumps, shovels of sand hurled at the burning timber in an effort to choke off the flames, pickaxes, and cant hooks to tear apart the burning piles or roll burning logs in the sand. Others were standing by in horror at their own helplessness or already running for their own houses to save what few belongings they could grab before the flames swept the buildings away. Within two hours after the fire had broken out, the Clintonville truck had raced the 38 miles over the winding country road, hub-deep in loose sand and gravel, to come roaring down the hillside into town, "the big engine singing like an airplane." For seventeen hours the truck pumped streams of water through 2,200 feet of hose, lifting it from the running stream 17 feet below its own level, before it had quenched the flames. Half of the lumberyard, though, and all the workers' homes had been saved.

In 1925 the company sold fire trucks to the cities of Hortonville and Crandon in Wisconsin and to Zion City, Illinois. In the next year they sold one to the city of Milwaukee, and before the year was out followed it with five more.

In 1928 they began a highly specialized adaptation of the motor truck to fire fighting in larger cities by developing and building twenty aerial-ladder tractors for the City of New York. These were so successful, with the added traction and power of the four-wheel drive, that other orders followed in succeeding years until by 1936 New York City had a fleet of sixty-eight FWD's. In that year came a new order for twelve aerial-ladder trucks—giants these, the largest ever built.

Specifications called for a special tractor and semitrailer, nearly 62 feet in over-all length, powered by a 150-horsepower engine, carrying 339 feet of ladders, among them an 85-foot suspension ladder, capable of being elevated and raised in less than 20 seconds to a full vertical position with a 200-pound weight on the extreme tip. The over-all weight of the completed truck was nearly 14 tons, with a speed of 45 to 50 miles an hour and the ability to climb or stop on a 17 per cent grade. For maneuvering in traffic and to turn the sharp corners of the city streets, the rear wheels under the trailer were capable of being steered separately from a tiller's seat just above them. So huge was the assembled truck that it was impossible to secure freight cars large enough and flatcars had to be converted into boxcars at the factory for their shipment. For the little factory in Clintonville to be building aerial-ladder trucks for the largest city in the country was an occasion of note, especially since the order had come in the midst of the depression, and Mr. Olen and other officials of the company were present for the final delivery and the dedication of the trucks in the open square in front of the city hall.

The ceremonies attracted a crowd of five thousand people and included a parade of fire-fighting equipment with its development over a period of twenty-five years. Firemen in the red uniforms of earlier days came in pulling the old hose reels, the ladder rack carts, and a hand pumper, which, with six men on a side pumping vigorously, spouted a stream of water twenty feet high and sixty feet in distance. Then came the three-horse-drawn steam-engine pumper, with the fire kindled, the steam up, and the whistle blowing. After that came the earlier motorized equipment, the ladder trucks and gasoline-engine-driven pumpers. Finally the twelve new FWD aerial-ladder trucks drove up in formation. The drivers dismounted, and the six-man crews took their places on the ladders. The captains released the foot pedals, and all ladders rose in unison to a full vertical position. Then the extension ladders moved upward to their full 85 feet, and while men climbed to the extreme tips, the turntables made a complete revolution. Then the ladders began their decline. In a brief ceremony the trucks were dedicated, by Monsignor William E. Coshin and the Reverend John McElligott, Jr., to the "service of saving life and property" in a city where 10,500 firemen and 400 pieces of equipment receive a call on the average of every ten minutes, or 56,738 yearly alarms. The pride of Mr. Olen and his fellow townsmen from Clintonville, however great on the occasion, may well be forgiven.

Similar aerial-ladder trucks went to the city of Boston within a few years and later, after the Second World War, a fleet of twelve, powered now with 240-horsepower engines, capable of reaching a speed of 30 miles per hour in 27 seconds from a standing start and able to make a complete turn in a 70-foot diameter, were delivered to the city of Chicago, and the Four Wheel Drive Auto Company of Clintonville was contributing to the fire protection of three of the largest cities of the country.

At the same time the big cities were calling for the giant, aerial-ladder trucks, smaller cities and towns and villages were calling for the single-unit pumpers and ladder and hose trucks of varying capacities. To meet the needs, the company developed triple-combination pumpers with capacities of 500 to 1,250 gallons, and trucks especially designed for rural areas, for with the development of the motorized fire truck a new era of fire protection was opened. No longer were small villages and rural township communities at the mercy of grass and forest fires, and no longer was it necessary for farm owners and neighbors, once fire had broken out, to stand helplessly by or to fall back on the primitive bucket brigade from pump and watering trough. By 1945 many states had passed special legislation encouraging fire-protective organizations in rural areas and small villages, supplementing local funds with state appropriations. Today the Four Wheel Drive fire truck is committed to the "service of saving life and property" in hundreds of areas and villages throughout the entire nation: in Staunton, Virginia, deep in the Shenandoah Valley and the Blue Ridge foothills; in Torrington, Connecticut, with its steep hillsides and sharp grades; in Fort Lauderdale, Florida, a city of sand, canals, and grassland; in Sauk Centre, Minnesota, in the heart of a dairyland where winter snow reaches a depth of 81 inches; in Dickinson, North Dakota, in a vast wheat and cattle area, with the world's largest beef auction, hub- and foot-deep in red, sticky gumbo after a rain; in a million acres of forest land in Oregon where the rain-drenched slopes and snow-covered areas of winter give way to a tinder-dry forest duff in late summer; in far away Anchorage, Alaska, a boom town of 31,000 with fewer than six city blocks of paved streets to lift it from bog and muskeg.

Sometimes indeed the Four Wheel Drive Auto Company and an industry utilizing the truck grew up together, as in the case of the Halliburton Oil Well Cementing Company, the world's largest operator in oil-field auxiliaries and today owner of the world's largest fleet of FWD trucks. Back in 1919, when Earle Halliburton, founder of the company, first began independent operation, the Four Wheel Drive Auto Company had just completed 16,000 trucks for the battle-fields of Europe. As a matter of fact, the first five trucks bought by Halliburton were war-surplus trucks sold by the U.S. Army at Fort Worth and Fort Sill in 1921.

Three years earlier, in 1919, after a youthful career as a railway construction worker, a steam-crane operator on the Mississippi, a sailor on tramp windjammers and in the merchant marine, an operator of a Navy motor barge during a period in the service, and an oil-field worker with the Perkins Oil Well Cementing Company, who had fired the young man for too many new ideas, Earle Halliburton had set up as an independent oil-well cementer. His first equipment had been a horse-drawn wagon, a borrowed pump, an old mixing tank, a clothesline for measuring depth, and some homemade plugs. With that he had managed to kill and cement-in a wild well for the Skelly Oil Company in the Hewitt oil field near Wilson, Oklahoma, and the next year, having invented a new jet mixer, and a sack cutter, as well as his own measuring device, he had increased his equipment to three wagons and was up at Fort Sill looking around for a speedier means of transportation.

Oil-well cementing work was then, and is today, almost always in the nature of an emergency. In the drilling of the well, or with the well already drilled and the shaft sunk, internal pressures far beneath the earth's surface are apt to blow out the shaft, frequently killing people and destroying property, sometimes opening a huge crater hundreds of feet in diameter where the drilling machinery once stood, and always, even without the surface damage, admitting water and gases into the well, disrupting the flow of oil, and corroding and plugging the pipes. In cementing a well the problem is to force a mixture of fluid concrete down the well shaft through the open pipe until it rises up between the shaft and the well wall to the strata where the pressures exist, and there, hardening, cuts off the flow or reinforces and protects the steel pipe. To force the cement down the shaft and up the well requires pressures of tremendous force. The earliest wells had been less than a hundred feet in depth and required pressures of 1,500 and 2,000 pounds per square inch; today wells of 13,000 to 14,000 feet in depth require pressures of up to 20,000 pounds per square inch and over.

The oil field itself always offers a difficult terrain. Over and over again the early vehicles had been stalled, sunk wagon-box-deep, or turned over and lost down some stony and cliff-edged hillside, or had to be abandoned in some bottomless bog, in the midst of marsh grass, bush, planking, and lopped tree limbs used for prying and leverage before the men had given up. The cementing trucks had to move in foul weather or fair, in rainstorms and cloudbursts, in the dry heat of a desert summer, or on the icy slopes of the mountains, and Mr. Halliburton found early that in buying the Four Wheel Drive trucks of the army surplus he had chosen wisely.

By 1924 Halliburton had a fleet of ten trucks and had incorporated his company with headquarters at Duncan, Oklahoma, for $350,000. In 1925, the first year of operation for the new company, he had cemented 270 wells. Ten years later, with an operating fleet of more than a hundred trucks, the company had cemented 80,000 wells, in a dozen different states. To the earlier cementing trucks, Halliburton had added new fleets, large, sturdy, powerful heavy-duty FWD's, capable of hauling massive boilers, and the heavy steel, timber, casing, and tubing of the drilling rigs. The Four Wheel Drive Auto Company, in addition to developing the heavy-duty cementing truck capable of the high pressures needed, working with Halliburton engineers had built a six-wheeled truck, equipped with a portable drilling rig, carrying a 90-foot telescoped derrick capable of drilling wells up to 4,000 feet, completely eliminating the need for the stationary wood or steel derrick that earlier dotted the oil-field landscape. Other trucks were engaged in hauling the materials, the steel and iron, the thousands of sacks of cement and gravel, and later the million tons of ready-mixed concrete, needed for the ever-increasing oil fields. To the service of cementing wells Halliburton had added a dozen others—oil-well testing, determining underground formations and their possible productivity while drilling and before casing and completing; oil-well acidizing, pumping in acids to dissolve limestone formations and to increase the flow; electrical well services, including the logging of underground formations by electric impulse, registering underground temperatures, perforating, and side-wall coring; and the process of Hydrafrac, an underground method of cracking or fracturing oil-bearing rock formations thousands of feet below the surface to restore flow in old wells.

By 1948 Four Wheel Drive units were cementing wells to record depths of 13,505 feet at Weeks Island in Louisiana and in Pecos County, Texas, a well to a depth of 15,270 feet, or approximately 3 miles below the surface. With eleven geographical divisions the Halliburton oil-well service was operating in nineteen states, with subsidiaries in Canada, Venezuela, and Peru, and FWD's were operating as far afield as Saudi Arabia, Kuwait, and Sumatra. The earliest cementer built by the Four Wheel Drive Auto Company had weighed 2,000 pounds; the latest, 22,000. The earliest one had cost $1,500, the later ones, $40,000, but the Halliburton Oil Well Cementing Company, organized in 1924 with a capital of $350,000, had grown to a company with a capital of $35,-000,000, a capital available, as Erle Halliburton has said, "to render a service to mankind and to earn a living for the men in our company."

What the big FWD heavy-duty trucks have meant to the oil-field operator is suggested by the story of a drilling contractor engaged in putting down a new well in a region so wild "the tool pusher needed a native guide to find the rig."

> We were two-thirds of the way up a mountain peak . . . with a steep slope breaking away in front of us. Three miles away and a thousand feet below one could see the trail winding towards us and upward. It wasn't much of an access road; we had just chopped down enough spruce to get through. We had been having tough weather, heavy rains, and the last one a regular Norther followed by a dip in the weather that had brought a two-inch coating of ice on the road and trails. On the way in—and the only way to get there that morning was by walking—we slipped, slid, rolled and crawled, inching our way upward.
>
> The drilling was tough, too. We were nearing oil formations and pockets of pressure would kick the tools around like toothpicks. She might let go. I've seen 'em do

it with less. When we got there the driller was sure jittery. He was down 7,580 feet and she had a big head on . . . there was a big show. He called down and the order had come to hold, cement, and then drill in. But would she hold, that was the question. It would be hours, maybe days before that ice gave way. You couldn't bring a cementer in on a pack trail, not even mules were that sure-footed. God Almighty!

There was a far off hum and then a roar down there in the valley, coming nearer, then threading between the spruce and juniper that lined the makeshift road, one could see the big red Halliburton-FWD cementer, with chains all around, crawling up there towards us on all fours. It gives a man goose pimples to see 'em come through just when a fellow needs 'em.

To the oil-well cementing company the FWD's have been the surest way of getting there "somehow safely," while to the Four Wheel Drive Auto Company the oil-well field has been a severe and consistent testing ground for new improvements and developments. It has been one of the best examples of two industries working hand in hand to meet cooperatively the needs of the market, the engineers of both companies concerned with a common problem, uniting the machine shop and laboratory.

Not alone for the Halliburton people but for a dozen different oil companies in hundreds of oil fields scattered throughout the country and the world, FWD's are hauling materials and digging wells in the ever-increasing demand for petroleum products, bringing in nearly 40,000 new wells a year.

In spite of the specialized uses and adaptations of the truck
to industrial needs, however, the primary function of a motor
truck was and has remained throughout its development
that of on-the-road and off-the-road hauling. A truck is a
carrying vehicle. Sooner or later, whenever the secondary
function of a motor-driven vehicle—digging, scraping, pushing, or lifting—has become primary, a highly specialized
machine has been built to meet the need—the bulldozer, the
power shovel, the motor grader, and hydraulic lifter, which
have in a sense replaced the truck itself. In 1917, when the
total truck registration was a little more than 300,000, nearly
all of them were used by the small owner for individual
hauling, from farm to market, from factory to retailer, and
from store to consumer. Twenty-five years later, in 1942,
with a truck registration of nearly five million, in spite of
the development of the fleet owner operating thousands of
trucks, more than half of the trucks were still individually
owned, and far more than half of them were still engaged

in farmer-to-market, factory-to-retailer, and store-to-customer hauling. An initial and continuing advantage of the FWD was its adaptability to both on-the-road and off-the-road service.

Among the first sales had been those to pickling and canning companies, where the ability to haul crops from the clay and sand of the cultivated fields, as well as to carry the loads over unimproved roads, was essential. Other sales had gone to the breweries of Appleton and Milwaukee, where the trucks, operating with heavy loads in the unimproved streets and alleys of the city, were equally capable of speeding along well-traveled intercity roads. One of the early purchasers had been Charles Hagen, later a director of the company, who had found an extensive and economic use for his Model B in operating a cheesebox factory in Black Creek and who wrote in 1914 as follows:

> The truck we bought last year has now travelled 31,320 miles on all kinds of roads. It has never been in a garage, or laid-up a single day. We get six miles on a gallon of gasoline, 467 miles on a gallon of oil. We figure it replaces six horse-wagons and the saving on oats and hay alone will pay for the truck.

Other early trucks had gone to the Silver City Beer and Ice Company of Denver, to the oil fields of the Inland Refining Company of Wyoming, to the Pacific Coast Condensed Milk Corporation, one of the first companies to adapt the motor truck to hauling liquids. And there were always the general contractors engaged in hauling machinery, gravel, supplies, and concrete, one of whom startled his fellow townsmen of Manchester, New Hampshire, when, having broken the rear axle in pulling out of a gravel pit, he rigged skids under the rear wheels and drove off with his front-wheel power pulling the load down the city streets.

The lumber industry, too, was one of the early ones attracted to the Four Wheel Drive. On the timbered slopes of steep hillsides or on a sandy, unimproved trail, and the ice- and snow-covered skid road, where earlier oxen and horse teams had skidded out, loaded, and drawn the logs to the mill, the trucks began operating with greater speed, heavier loads, and equal sure-footedness. In 1925, 234 sawmills in the state of Wisconsin were still sawing more than a billion feet a year. On the Menominee Indian Reservation, with its twenty-three logging camps, Four Wheel Drive trucks were hauling as high as 3,564 feet of hardwood logs, weighing more than 24 tons to the load. Within another decade Four Wheel Drives were operating in the lumber camps of northern Michigan, in the states of Wyoming and Florida, and in the deep snows and icy winters of the Canadian northwoods. For the Newaygo Lumber Corporation of Canada the horse-drawn load of three cords of pulpwood with one 10-mile haul per day had given way to FWD's, which, with two sleds attached, were hauling 22 cords per load and capable of making six to seven trips in the 10-hour day. In Wyoming an FWD, drawing one sled, brought in over 650 railway ties daily over a 3½-mile haul. In Kenora, Ontario, five FWD's owned by the Ontario-Minnesota Pulp and Paper Company set a record in hauling pulp logs out of the woods to Red Cliff Bay, by carrying a load and drawing two sleds up and down the steep grades and over the ice of the lake, with a payload of 50 tons, or 375 cords per day. In Ocala, Florida, heavy-duty Model HA's were hauling up to 17,000 feet of longleaf pine, the trucks plowing their way through 5 miles of ball-bearing sand and gravel.

Two decades later the Crossett Lumber Company of Arkansas was using 200-horsepower FWD diesel truck-and-trailer combinations equipped with twenty forward and four reverse speeds, capable of traveling at legal speed limits with a load of 3,000 to 5,000 board feet, a gross combined-weight load of 75,000 pounds. Other heavy-duty FWD's were logging in the Cache National Forest of Utah; in the Wallawa National Forest in Oregon, where the 50-mile road switches around in hairpin curves over the Blue Mountains; in bog, sand, and mud of the tidewater swamps of South Carolina.

Especially adapted to both on-the-road and off-the-road hauling, Four Wheel Drive trucks were early used in the sugar camps of the Kiawiki Sugar Corporation on the island of Ookala in Hawaii, in the pineapple fields of Oahu and Malchai, and in the sugarcane fields of Cuba, the trucks plowing their way easily through the wet, marshy fields and over the unimproved roads. Early in the thirties the Davey Tree Company of Ohio, operating in thirty-five states and in Canada, began to use FWD's in transplanting trees, some of them more than a hundred years old and 28 inches in diameter, the trucks moving through plowed field and pasture, over fill and newly graded lawn and the ice-covered roads of a winter-centered operation. Especially designed for the truck was a 20,000-pound power winch used for breaking the bole of the tree from the earth, lowering it onto a multiwheeled trailer, and later erecting and lowering the tree into the newly dug hole. Down in Tennessee a fleet of FWD's was hauling steel for the 325-foot towers of the TVA power lines from the Joe Wheeler dam to Columbia, a 350-mile route of muddy lanes and rough countryside. Far up north, within the Arctic Circle another fleet was hauling supplies to the mines over the ice and snow and muskeg from the Eldorado Mining and Refining Company on Great Bear Lake.

In 1932 a $40,000,000 pipeline was laid from the Mediterranean coast over 675 miles of trackless wastes where no wheeled vehicles had ever gone before into the interior of Iraq to tap the great oil fields of the Middle East. To bring in the materials, Four Wheel Drive trucks, pulling four-wheeled trailers and hauling 30 tons of steel per truck, beat out a highway from Cairo in Egypt to Kirkuk in Assyria, across the burning sands of the desert in temperatures ranging as high as 120 degrees. By 1950 the Arabian Motor Car Company had a fleet of more than fifty FWD trucks, engaged in the general transport of merchant cargo, over a route reaching from Jidda to Mecca, a short stretch of macadamized road, and thence onward for a thousand miles over old camel routes, across salt flats and lava rock formations, through the desert sands of Medina, Taif, and Riyadh.

Specializing in off-and-on-the-road service, and going, indeed, where no roads are at all, the Four Wheel Drive trucks have steadily moved forward to the far corners of the world. With an equal ability for economy and speed of operation and with far greater safety on four-wheel traction and less vulnerability to skidding than a conventional rear-drive, they have demonstrated an equal capacity for over-the-road hauling. The earliest trucks ever sold had been used for farm-to-market hauling and for intercity hauling by the canning companies and breweries. In the late twenties and thirties and into the forties and fifties, thousands of later FWD's had joined the nearly 9 million trucks rolling over the streets and highways of America and bringing ever-widening markets to farmers, a thousand new services to city dwellers, and transforming the life of a thousand communities that have no freight connection with the outside world except that of the motor truck. Of the 9 billion tons of domestic freight in 1946, 5 billion tons, especially in local hauling, went by motor truck. Of the 4 billion tons of intercity hauling, more than one-sixth was moved by motor truck alone. In that year the farmers of America were operating more than 2 million trucks, in addition to 24,000 commercial fleets of eight trucks or more, employing a contingent of 5½ million men. By 1952 a single intercity transfer line in the Middle West, operating in an area of less than 350 miles in diameter, had rung up nearly 25 million miles, the equivalent of encircling the earth a thousand times, with individual FWD's in the fleet having operated in more than one million accident-free miles.

An interesting aspect of the transportation story has been the relation of the motor truck to the railroads. In the early days it was the assumed task of the motor truck to supplement the railroads, bringing supplies to shipping centers and carrying the freight from depot to markets and consumers. In the twenties had come an adaptation of the motor truck to the railroad itself, when a Model B, equipped with flanged wheels, replaced the steam engine for the New Orleans and Lower Coast Road in Louisiana. Other experiments with the Four Wheel Drive trucks as engine power took place in California, Iowa, and as far away as China. Down in West Virginia, a Model B built in 1925, equipped with a streetcar body, still operated in 1945 as the sole train on 19 miles of railroad from Buffalo Creek to Wyden, carrying seats for sixteen passengers and ample room for local freight, over "the twistingest, crookedest road in existence," with seven flag stops and a ten-minute holdover at Swandale. In 1947 a new fleet of FWD's shipped to China by UNRRA were being outfitted as railroad locomotives for the China National Railroad, running from Canton to Hengyang, a distance of 450 miles, pulling three standard 40-foot boxcars.

Although motor-truck motive power has been substituted for the locomotive on its own roadbed, the motor truck has in the long run rivaled the railway itself with its transportation over the public highway. By 1942, for instance, 85 per cent of the milk hauled to large cities throughout the United States went by motor truck; more than 4,500,000 cases of eggs rolled into Chicago annually via the motor truck, plus another 58,000,000 pounds of poultry; nearly 69 per cent of all cattle shipped and 40 per cent of all fruits and vegetables to the major markets of the country went by motor truck. Drawing from a 200-mile radius, the market of New York City alone today receives 1,600 truckloads of produce on a single night, with 5,000 additional truck trips required to distribute the night's receipts to city stores. Out of a total of 125,617 communities in the United States, 54,453, or 43 per cent, are served by motor truck alone.

Indeed, the highways and motor trucks have not only transformed the scene of America; they have transformed the living habits and diets of 150,000,000 people. Rolling northward out of Florida, eastward over the Rockies, up from the Deep South of the Rio Grande, down from the apple country of Oregon, and outward from the orchards of Colorado and Michigan and in from the Great Plains, their deep bins loaded with fruits and vegetables, their stock racks filled with cattle and sheep and the hogs of Iowa and Illinois, motor trucks from every state are engaged in a vast movement supplying the dinner tables of North, East, West, and South, bringing to them an abundance and variety unknown to the American people in any earlier period.

Even before the Second World War, Four Wheel Drive trucks were operating throughout the world: hauling freight for the Sourdough Express in Fairbanks, Alaska, pulpwood in the Northern forests of Canada, oil-well equipment in the deserts of Saudi Arabia and on the island of Madagascar; pulling combines in the wheat harvest of Kansas; hauling sugar and cane in Hawaii, rubber in Java, freight and passengers in Hongkong, hides and wool on the pampas of Argentina, ore in Mexico and Guatemala, steel in Egypt and Syria, coffee in Yemen, cement in Stockholm and Holland. In England and Spain, in France and Germany, in Ireland and Wales, in Russia and Africa, in the Philippines and Australia, in Honduras and the Barbados, in Venezuela, Colombia, Ecuador, Brazil and Bolivia, in Chile and Peru, on Martinique and Malta, in Algeria and Romania, Greece, Palestine, Abyssinia, Rhodesia, in Persia and India, in Ceylon, Guam, Tasmania, and New Zealand, on nearly every island and on every continent known to civilized men.

If such, however, has been the story of the motor truck and some of its major developments in the heavy-duty line in the decades between two wars, it is not the full story of the Four Wheel Drive Auto Company itself. By 1925, fol-

lowing the slump in the truck market immediately succeeding the First World War, seventy truck manufacturing companies had failed and were in the hands of receivers or in
bankruptcy. That the Four Wheel Drive Auto Company did
not succumb is due primarily to the tenacity and vision of
its directors and to the rapidity with which the Four Wheel
Drive truck was adapted to meet changing conditions and
new demands. The four-wheel-drive principle was basically
sound engineering. The Model B, for all its limitations, was
a sound and sturdy vehicle, and if the original gift of the
Federal government to the state highway departments and
to the Federal parks had brought about its widespread use
throughout the country, it was the ability of the engineers
and the foresight of the board of directors, led by W. A.
Olen, that had kept the company going.

For five years, from 1920 onward, the company spent between $30,000 and $40,000 a year in free servicing of the
20,000 Model B's in operation in the highway departments,
in the hands of other government bureaus and private contractors, though not until 1924 did it make any sale of new
trucks to the highway departments. When in 1923 it had
secured the rights for building the International earth-boring
machine and had mounted it on Four Wheel Drive trucks,
the redesigning of the truck to meet the demands of the
power and traction needed involved a loss of nearly $600 a
truck for the first five units. Then the company bought the
International earth borer outright, and after developing a
new five-speed transmission and contracting with Western
Electric for the mounting of Spowart borers as well, utility
orders had gone up from one truck in 1924 to nearly 2,000
in 1925. In 1923 it had engineered the first snowplow

mounted on a Model B and in the next five years developed a general road maintainer combining the snowplow and underbody scraper. It had assumed tasks of fundamental engineering in oil-field work and in the fire truck, and in half a dozen other motor-truck fields.

All of this had represented huge expenditures without any immediate visible returns, but by 1926 it began to be clear that the company had weathered its most difficult years. For that year sales reached a total of $1,691,743, with a sale of spare parts of $61,385 and a payroll of 402 workers. By 1928 the total sales reached over $2,000,000, and for the first time since the war the company's annual statement showed an operating profit of $109,000.

"What was this company organized for anyway?" one of the irate stockholders had asked the year before at the annual meeting. "I figured it was to make money, and if we continue to pay out dividends as we have been doing and reduce the money we got in war bonds, and still don't make any money, what are we coming to in the end, I'd like to know."

And the answer had not been easy. You had to keep on paying dividends, small ones, 3 to 6 per cent (which they had done every year except for 1922 and 1923), to keep the stockholders interested and in the business, the president replied. It was true the war-surplus funds were dwindling. You had to keep investing in new tools and machinery, and the experimental work in developing new trucks and new adaptations was costing a lot of money, but if they could be patient, it would pay off in the end. During the past six years 44 per cent of all corporations had been operating at a loss and 29 per cent had showed a profit of less than $2,000;

19 per cent of them less than $10,000; and only 8 per cent a profit of more than $100,000. "We'll move up into that class in another year or so," he concluded.

And the company had. In the following year, 1929, they did even better. In that year the total sales reached $3,296,-564, or an increase of 31 per cent and a net operating profit of $213,000. They were employing a working force of 768 employees, working in two shifts. They were building trucks now for the highways, the public-utility companies, oil fields, and the general contractor. They were engaged in building twenty-four new 5-ton trucks for the government. Unfortunately it was the best year the company was to have for another decade.

At the annual meeting of the company in 1931, they had been in business exactly twenty years. During that time they had manufactured and marketed some 25,000 trucks. They had developed and engineered a line of heavy-duty trucks, ranging from the lighter-weight 2-ton to 7½- and 10-ton vehicles. During the twenty years they had paid out over $9,000,000 to the workers in Clintonville and the surrounding farming country. They had paid out nearly $2,000,000 in cash dividends to the stockholders, most of them Clintonville residents, and well over $1,000,000 in stock dividends. They had paid out more than $5,500,000 in local, state, and Federal taxes. During the twenty years the number of workers employed had varied from 100 to 1,600, but the company had never been shut down a single day either by strike or for want of business. During exactly the same twenty years more than a hundred firms and individuals had failed in trying to manufacture a successful four-wheel-drive vehicle. In the current year, however, sales declined over $1,000,000 from the high point of 1929, and operating profit dwindled to $141,000. Sales in the utility field alone dropped from $613,499 to $288,886. It was a prelude for a new decade of struggle and survival—the depression era of the thirties.

In his annual report to the stockholders, W. A. Olen cited the failure of 1,324 banks during the year, tying up nearly a billion dollars, as a kind of ominous warning. Four years earlier, the company, studying its own records and procedures in consultation with financial experts, particularly with reference to selling on time and to allowing excessive trade-in values, had sharply reorganized its own practice and restricted itself to a cash basis. It had been a singularly farsighted move. Without any indebtedness, without any preferred stock, without any contingent liabilities, and with still a $200,000 reserve in Federal bonds, the company was as ready as any to meet the uncertainties of the future. Its first effort would be to meet the crisis head on with a yearly advertising campaign of nearly $100,000 and a redoubled effort on the part of its salesmen, who were already making nearly 60,000 personal calls a year at an average cost of $5.

In spite of every effort, however, sales dropped off steadily. In 1931 they declined to a little more than $2,000,000, a drop of 28 per cent from the previous year. In 1932 they declined to a little more than $1,000,000, a decrease of 45 per cent, with an operating loss for the year of $148,171. Wages had been reduced 18 per cent and salaried employees had taken a cut of 28 per cent. In the face of the declining market, inventories had been reduced 15 per cent and general expenses had been reduced by $32,000. To offset the financial loss involved, $30,000 worth of trucks had been repossessed. To liquidate an account in South America, Joe

Cotton spent an entire year closing out an account of $63,000, at a cost of $12,000 collecting $17,000. During the year W. A. Olen traveled 30,000 miles, covering forty-two states, supervising and checking on the organization of dealers, salesmen, and branch offices, interviewing customers and prospective buyers. In the face, however, of 1,200 men and women in the city of Clintonville already unemployed, the company had been forced to reduce the number on its payroll. "It is always difficult for management to retreat properly and to do it intelligently and humanely," Mr. Olen reported to the stockholders.

> In times such as these the most important task for our company is to provide work for its employees. Nevertheless we have been forced to drop 279 men and women from our payroll. We have done this reluctantly and not without concern for their welfare. In every case we have followed through and tried to secure other employment for them, or we have seen them resettled on farms or in other jobs to see that they have means of support.
>
> It is times such as we went through last year that really test the fibre of our organization, the stockholders, the employees, the customers, and even the entire community. . . . It is difficult for men to work under these conditions, but the morale has been holding up surprisingly well, and I believe the men will continue to face the situation courageously, sensibly and efficiently.

It was in the year ahead, however, in 1933, that the depression was to reach its depth. In that year sales dropped to a bare $1,000,000 and the foreign market declined to $12,000. Early in the year both Clintonville banks closed, tying up all operating funds, as well as all funds to meet the current pay checks of the company already issued. For the support of its salesmen in the field the company wired the Continental Bank of Illinois to express $4,000. An hour later every bank in the country was closed for a national moratorium by presidential decree. For its own employees the company began to issue script exchangeable in local stores for groceries and the minimum necessities.

During the last two years, as W. A. Olen reported to the stockholders at the annual meeting in January of 1934, more than 100,000 corporations had failed and 100,000 manufacturing concerns had had to shut down entirely, at a loss to the national economy of $3,000,000,000. In 1932, 7,000 banks had closed their doors before the national moratorium; 20,000 people had committed suicide; in 1933 the number had reached 35,000. But their own company had managed to keep going, and though operating at a loss, it had given employment to nearly 500 people and paid out $372,930 in wages. It had had to turn down an offer of a neighboring city to buy thirteen trucks amounting to $85,000 because the city could pay only in bonds, with a debt already amounting to $39,000,000, and the city unable to collect a third of its taxes. Three years earlier the utility field had accounted for 35 per cent of the total business of the company. This year not one truck had been sold to the entire utility field.

In August of that year the NRA had gone into effect, asking for a general increase in the hourly rates for labor and in a decrease of the working week from 45 and 50 hours to 36. It was easy to sympathize with the general design of the act to spread the work out among the workers and to bolster the economy by increasing the money in the hands of the laboring class, but to a company already operating at a loss, instead of paying one man for a 44-hour week at 25 cents an hour, a total of $11, it meant paying one man for a 36-hour week at the hourly rate of 40 cents, and hiring a second man for the other 8 hours, at a total cost for the two of $17.60. It was difficult to see how this would help the local situation; one could only trust it might some way benefit the over-all situation and so result in a general recovery that might help the company.

To the average stockholder in Clintonville, concerned with securing dividends to pay his own taxes, the argument seemed fallacious, but something may be said for him, too. One of them spoke up from the floor:

> I want to say that I have learned a great deal today, not only about this industry but others, in the way of figures that have been presented. I need cash to pay my taxes, too, but I move we leave the question of dividends to the directors. I can't help but feel that we have been exceedingly fortunate. We have kept our overhead down; we have given employment to laboring people. We have kept going . . . I think Clintonville is to be congratulated.

Certainly the spirit of the stockholders themselves helped to maintain company morale.

During the next year sales slowly increased. By 1935 they had risen to $3,000,000, and the worst of the depression was over; by 1938 they had risen to more than $4,000,000. Employment had increased from a low of 328 to more than 900. The Walsh-Healey Act had stabilized the 40-hour week, with time and a half for overtime on all government orders of more than $10,000. The National Labor Relations Board had recognized the rights of collective bargaining, and established unemployment insurance and old-age pensions, liability, sickness, and accident insurance for the worker. In 1937, in an agreement with the company union, wages had been increased by 50 per cent. Partly to offset the higher cost in wages, the company had spent $200,000 in modernizing the factory, in improving buildings, tools, machines, and equipment. By 1938 the high crest of recovery had been reached, and the recession of '38 and '39 was at hand. Once more sales dropped from the high of $4,000,000 in 1938 to $2,000,000 in 1939, with foreign sales dropping again, from $588,980 to $111,014.

As W. A. Olen explained to the stockholders at the annual meeting in September, 1938,

> Our problems have been no different from those of other industries throughout the nation, with perhaps this exception, that many other companies instead of granting the increase in pay and cutting down to the forty hour week, proposed to fight it out with a result that there were strikes and lockouts, and war between capital and labor and an ill feeling which it takes years and years to overcome. Our employees are distinctly friendly. They have adopted methods provided by law . . . but in a spirit of friendliness and cooperation.
>
> The most valuable asset we have is our thousands of satisfied customers and the hundreds of men and women in our company who have lived through good times and bad, who know how to work together. . . . Our finances are in splendid shape, our factory is rebuilt and reorganized, our labor organization is willing to cooperate . . . our house is in order to live through this recession and to meet the future—the new return of business that will surely come.

And the return again came but not until—and there are those who say not without—the stimulus to American industry of a second world war. In the spring of 1939 came Hitler's march into Austria and the Anschluss; in August the German armies began the invasion of Poland. In 1940 sales suddenly rose to more than $6,000,000. A second world war was already engulfing America. Late that year a member of an organization representing small business had come to Clintonville to look over the factory, interview the management, and ask the company to join their organization. He had asked for the annual statement and had studied it carefully. "I am sorry," he had said to Mr. Olen, terminating the interview, "but I cannot ask you to join our organization. You no longer belong to small business. No one can belong to our organization whose capitalization is $2,000,000, whose stock is listed on the stock exchange, and who is doing a business of $5,000,000 a year."

The statement startled Walter A. Olen. In thirty years since the day he and Otto Zachow and William Besserdich had gone up and down the streets of Clintonville trying to organize the new company . . . in thirty years, through near failure, through a world-war boom, through the periodic recessions of the twenties and the thirties, they had hung on. They were no longer a small business, but a small business that had become big.

Skidding and Slewing

That the four-wheel-drive principle was sound engineering in terms of power and tractional ability had been demonstrable from the very first. The company's $1,000 challenge in the case of the original car, that no rear-driven car could follow it for twenty minutes through a selected terrain, was never claimed or collected, though essayed in the early days by literally hundreds of different makes. The truck's superior ability in on-and-off-the-road service had remained uncontested among thousands of trucks delivered for military service and thousands later employed in the highway and utility fields. On all fours it could outpull ox teams or mule teams or horse-drawn wagons or any rear-driven trucks. It was equally at ease in plowed field, or sand, or loose gravel, or on a steep grade. It was less subject to fatigue and strain, more economical, capable of infinitely greater speed than ox or mule team or horses, and, with the later developments in horsepower and greater sturdiness of construction, of infinitely greater power. A second factor claimed for the early

Four Wheel Drive truck, that it was also safer than a rear-drive, was less easily demonstrable.

That safety, however, as well as power, had been one of the original concerns is attested to by nearly all the early patent claims. "The slipping of drive wheels on muddy or sandy roads or in hill climbing or skidding and sideslip when running an incline or in making abrupt turns" was one of the hazards the four-wheel-drive principle was to preclude. To prove that it did so and to demonstrate the driver's absolute power over the vehicle, one of Walter A. Olen's favorite stunts in the early days was to have the truck driven up the concrete steps of the Lutheran church in Clintonville, and then to have it back down again, holding and reversing, one step at a time. To show his complete confidence in the tractional ability and the braking power of the four wheels, he would place his open-face gold watch on a step under the front wheel and ask the driver to begin the descent and to hold the truck with the front wheel poised and resting just above the watch, before the truck pulled ahead again permitting the owner to retrieve it. "I never lost a watch," Mr. Olen will still tell you proudly.

In 1920, after some 20,000 trucks, manufactured for European countries or the United States Army, had been released to the state highway departments or sold to private contractors as army surplus, a criticism of the truck among unpracticed drivers was that the Four Wheel Drive trucks were difficult to steer. All trucks equipped with solid rubber tires were difficult to steer in uneven terrain, and the heavier the truck the greater the difficulty; but the Four Wheel Drive was less so, Walter A. Olen was convinced, than the conventional rear-drive. In the latter the front wheels, which were always in the process of being pushed around, allowed for sideslip and digging in and cramping; in the Four Wheel Drive the front wheels pulled themselves around under their own power, without digging in or sideslipping. The real difficulty lay with the driver who sought to impose direction on his wheels without waiting for the power of the wheels to pull themselves around.

To demonstrate the ease with which an experienced driver could handle the truck, the company selected a young woman, Luella Bates, from among its own test drivers during the war and sent her to the New York Auto Show. Two years earlier, because of manpower shortage, the company had employed 150 young women as drivers, testing each truck in a 75-mile run, before shipping or delivering it. Miss Bates weighed 130 pounds, but, dressed in an Oxford-gray uniform, puttees, and a jaunty overseas cap, as one of the New York papers recorded it, could handle the 3-ton truck "as if it were a tricycle." Having demonstrated for the auto-show people by driving through the most congested areas of the city, Miss Bates was later sent on a transcontinental trip in the interests of a Safety-First, Drive for Children Campaign sponsored by Francis H. Hugo, then Secretary of State.

It was only one of many attempts the company made to stress safety. At the annual meeting of the stockholders in 1924, Walter A. Olen spoke at length about the highway-building program, its extent and cost, the increased traffic, and the danger involved to human life. "We manufacture a truck to operate on streets and highways," he exclaimed,

> and we owe it to the public which builds and maintains them, to furnish a truck that will take up the least room, that will do the least damage to the highways and streets,

The Four Wheel Drive race car, winner of the Equinox Mountain Hill Climb and the Edenvale Airport run. "It is something to ponder that there are performance regions in speed, acceleration, and climbing ability which are forever beyond the two-wheel-drive machine regardless of its design perfection. . . ."

. . . on the timbered slopes of hillsides, over the oxen and horse-trod skid roads, with greater speed, heavier loads, and equal sure-footedness. . . .

. . . within a decade the motor truck snow-plow had practically equalized winter and summer driving. . . .

. . . on the level road, in the ditches along the side, up the mountain
pass, over boulder and cliff where no highway ascends . . . to meet the
needs of flowing power.

. . . night and day, in bad weather and good, and always where a heavy duty truck is in demand. . . .

. . . contributing to the
fire protection of the
largest cities of America.

OPPOSITE: . . . only the huge rotaries with six-foot
augers and the whirling fan of the blower spewing
aside a 100-foot plume of snow can eat their way
through.

OPPOSITE: World War II. On scores of landing beaches, in dozens of rebuilt harbors, on hundreds of hastily built airfields and bases, over thousands of miles of unimproved and rebuilt highways, the FWD's helped carry on the endless burden of supply.

The giant, 20-ton, six-wheel-drive crane carrier built for the Army Engineers—powerful enough to go anywhere—operating in Korea, on a hundred air bases in North Africa and the wide Pacific, in the flooded lowlands along the Missouri and Mississippi.

The earliest cementer weighed 2,000 pounds, the latest 22,000. The earliest wells were less than a hundred feet in depth, the latest 15,270 feet, or nearly three miles below the surface . . . one of the best examples of two industries working hand in hand . . . uniting the machine shop and the laboratory.

OPPOSITE: In 1938 Otto Zachow and Walter A. Olen rehearse the early days. Otto retires as a machinist and the company acquires the Machine Shop, site of the original invention of the four-wheel drive.

The Four Wheel Drive Auto Company, 1952 . . . no longer a small business, but a small business that has become big.

. . . in hundreds of oil fields scattered
throughout the country and the world,
FWD's are hauling materials and digging wells in the ever-increasing demand
for petroleum products, bringing in nearly
40,000 new wells a year.

Pine Lake, near Clintonville, scene of winter driving tests. "What has become clearly evident is that winter driving hazards in the states of the snow belt can be directly reduced by the application of motor power to all wheels of a vehicle."

The FWD in World War II. "Probably the greatest unsung military supply wagon of the war was the army truck."

In England, FWD trucks equipped with the utility field earth borer dug out ten thousand delayed-action bombs dropped by German war planes.

The Alcan Highway built by FWD's across 1,480 miles of a vaguely mapped virgin wilderness of mountain streams, swamps, bog, and muskeg.

FWD's in over-the-road hauling . . . with an equal ability for economy and speed, far greater safety, and less vulnerability to skidding. . . .

. . . dedicated to the saving of life and property . . .

and that will at all times be under the best control of the driver.

To augment the program, he had early begun to collect all newspaper reports of accidents involving skidding or slewing. By 1930 he had collected thousands of them, and, convinced that a great percentage of accidents actually took place on good roads, many of them on pavements, and involved vehicular control on curves or under uncertain road conditions, he was ready to launch a more extensive program.

Fundamentally convinced that the four-wheel-drive principle was a strategic factor in safety and vehicular control, the company still faced the problem of convincing the public. To state the claim in advertising would be to have it discounted by the public or met by counterclaims for rear-wheel drives by other advertisers. Demonstration, however, becomes an incontestable truth. And whether or not it was actually true could only be tested by field conditions. Other manufacturers in the automobile world, men like Ford and Firestone, were testing their products by subjecting them to the grueling run of the Indianapolis automobile derby. Two-thirds of all new ideas and engineering innovations in motors and body construction, in wheels and size of tires, in oils and gasolines, were given their initial tests there. Why not try out a Four Wheel Drive car on the Indianapolis track?

In 1930 W. A. Olen persuaded the board of directors to let a contract with Harry Miller, dean of racing-car builders, for the engineering and construction of an FWD race car, embodying the basic principles of the Four Wheel Drive truck. The car was completed early in 1932 and shipped to Indianapolis just in time for the race that year. To attend the initial run, W. A. Olen and the board of directors left for Indianapolis by train. Bill Smith, one of the drivers at the plant, drove the old scout car, *Nancy Hanks,* to Indianapolis to celebrate the event and to dramatize the four-wheel-drive principle, still in all its essentials basically what it had been twenty years earlier when the FWD under Captain Williams had come through on the Washington–Fort Benjamin Harrison test run.

Unfortunately the race car arrived at the track too late for thorough testing. At the time it was powered by a V-8 motor developing 300 horsepower and capable of speeds in excess of 175 miles per hour. For the race the car was managed by Barney Oldfield and Harry Miller and driven by Bob McDonough. In the opening runs it qualified at 117 miles per hour. During the big race faulty lubrication developed excessive motor heating, and the car was withdrawn after the seventh lap. For the time being W. A. Olen and the board of directors had to content themselves with the general curiosity the car aroused and with Bob McDonough's comment that on the slippery track, well-greased from the seeping lubricants of seventy-five racers, the car handled easily and deftly enough to be driven by a child.

For the next three years ill luck dogged every effort. In 1933, the car, driven by Frank Brisko, was roaring along at 150 miles per hour before it was again forced to the pit because of motor trouble. In 1934 the V-8 motor had been replaced with a four-cylinder engine. Brisko drove it once more, leading the field for the first 177 miles, relinquishing the lead, and regaining it again at 280 miles.

It had earlier been a common belief that a four-wheel-drive car because of its weight was inevitably slower than a rear-drive. At 277 miles when Brisko had received a sign from the pit to pass No. 9 and did so in less than two laps, passing on the turn at 143 miles per hour, the feat brought thousands of spectators to their feet. The car held the road safely. For well over the first half of the race Brisko averaged 104.64 miles per hour. Then the overflow pipe from the oil tank broke and sprayed the driver with hot oil, blistering driving hands and forcing a reduction in speed. At 322 miles Brisko came into the pit and Rex May, a relief driver, took over, driving four laps and 10 miles before discovering how to shift into high gear and finally finishing in ninth place for an average speed of 96.7 miles per hour.

In the next two years the car was driven by Mauri Rose. In the 1935 race, starting in the tenth position, Rose had moved forward to third place at 177 miles, averaging more than 108 miles per hour, when he was forced out of the race by a broken stud in the water manifold. In the 1936 race, entered against twenty-five rear- and five front-drives, the car made its best single showing at the Indianapolis track. That year its starting position was thirteenth and Rose finished the race in fourth place. What had cost him the victory was a refueling stop on the 121st lap. All cars that year had been limited to 37½ gallons of gasoline, to 6 gallons of oil, and to gasoline tanks containing no more than 15 gallons. Fearing that he might run out before the finish, Rose had stopped to refuel. The three cars ahead of him had driven through, the winner finishing with less than a pint of gasoline in the tank.

To Walter A. Olen and the other officials of the company

who had gone down for the race it was something of a heartbreaking experience. It would have been a notable event to have had the Four Wheel Drive car actually win the race. Winning, however, was less important than the accumulation of demonstrable facts about speed, and safety, and the ease of handling, and of factors relating, too, to the economy of a Four Wheel Drive. Any four-wheel-drive principle adds extra mechanism to a car and increases the over-all weight. The Four Wheel Drive racing car generally outweighed its competitors by 300 pounds. Conceded to be the fastest single car at the track, the Four Wheel Drive had also established enviable records in economy and in tire wear.

More significant, however, were the testimonies of the drivers and mechanics to its ease of handling, its superior traction on oily and slippery tracks, its effective acceleration and getaway without wheel spinning, its safety on turns and curves, which though taken at higher speeds were without skidding or rear-end whip. "I want to say," Mauri Rose had replied to a reporter from the Indianapolis *Times*, concluding an interview, "that I have never driven a car or a truck that had the safety of steering or the traction to compare with the Four Wheel Drive car." "The important thing is that I can drive at high speed over the rough oily track with safety," Frank Brisko testified in 1933. "I can go through curves without any tendency of the car to weave." "It is my idea of a racing car," Barney Oldfield had written after managing it in 1932. "I drove your car in a practice spin and it handled wonderfully." "It is now one of the fastest, if not the fastest car in the course," the reporter for the Indianapolis *News* had written. "The Four Wheel Drive is ideal for getting around curves."

It was not, however, until 1950 and later—if one may get ahead of the story—that the Four Wheel Drive car demonstrated its incontestable superiority in a series of road races and hill-climbing competitions. For this work the Indianapolis racing car was loaned in 1948 to William F. Milliken, Jr., of the Cornell Aeronautical Laboratory for an informal program of research which sought understanding of four-wheel-drive behavior in critical conditions, as well as further knowledge of necessary balance and design for optimum performance. Mr. Milliken, manager of the Flight Research Department, and his associates had independently reached the conclusion that for high-powered vehicles operating under limiting traction conditions and extreme side loads during cornering, four-wheel-drive power offered the greatest promise. To confirm their conclusions, which were largely based on theoretical considerations and the known shortcomings of high-powered rear-driven cars, they were eager to test the Four Wheel Drive car in actual field conditions and under thorough competition.

Under Mr. Milliken's management the Four Wheel Drive car was entered in a variety of racing events sponsored by the Sports Car Club of America and by the American Automobile Association, where the car was driven under as widely diverse conditions as those of Pikes Peak, Watkins Glen, the Edenvale Airport run, and the Equinox Mountain Hill Climb. Basically designed for the level-track competition of the Indianapolis derby and without any basic modification in suspension, brakes, and transmission or power-weight ratio for the more specialized conditions of road racing or hill climbing, the car consistently showed a superiority in acceleration and cornering speed over the best competition.

Never once, though subjected to every severity of cornering on a dozen types of road surfaces and driven by amateur drivers, was the car involved in an accident which would reflect adversely on its handling characteristics. In the 1950 national competition at the Equinox Mountain Hill Climb in Vermont, the Four Wheel Drive car came away a clear winner, establishing a new national record for hill-climbing ability.

The Equinox Mountain race, sponsored by the Sports Car Club of America, covers 6¼ miles of steep winding and twisting mountain road, with frequent gradients of 14 per cent. Equinox Mountain comprises two peaks, the lower one at 2,720 feet above the starting level and the second one rising 496 feet higher, with two sets of switchbacks and hairpin turns, one just below the summit of Little Equinox and the second just short of the top of the higher peak, where the approach is sufficiently steep to cut off the view and the direction of the road ahead.

Sixteen cars had been entered in the race, fifteen started, and twelve finished. The chief competition of the day was between the Four Wheel Drive car, driven by William Milliken, Jr., and a Grand Prix type of rear-driven Maserati, handled by George Weaver, winner of the Seneca Cup Race at Watkins Glen in 1949. On its first timed ascent, the Four Wheel Drive made the run in 7 minutes and 14 seconds for an average speed of 52 miles per hour. The initial run of the Maserati made the 6¼ miles in 7 minutes and 8 seconds. On the second run Milliken held to the outside on the hairpin turns, cutting sharply across to the inside of the curve, and then again to the outside, accelerating on the turn. Approaching the summit of Little Equinox at 70 miles an hour, coming up over the rise and out onto the ridge with nothing but the blue sky ahead, was a sensation, he said later, never to be forgotten. When the second and third gears seemed to be stripped, he shifted into first and roared up the last ascent, for a total elapsed time of 6 minutes and 59 seconds, or an average speed of 54.2 miles per hour. The previous hill-climbing record had been 48.2 miles per hour, a speed established by Lewis Unser on the 7 per cent grade, Pikes Peak Highway, in the Labor Day race of 1946.

In the spring of 1952 the car was again entered in a series of races comprising the Edenvale Airport event. Here the conditions were quite different from those of Equinox Mountain and other mountain hill climbs. The surface was hard, dry macadam and the circuit such that considerably higher speeds could be reached. It did not seem likely that the four-wheel-drive principle would offer a great advantage on a circuit of such basically excellent tractive conditions or that a car designed and built twenty years earlier could equal the accelerative ability of modern rear-drives. The principal competition at the event was a new J-2X Allard, powered with one of the best Cadillac racing engines in this country. In every respect—brakes, power, weight, suspension, and transmission—the Allard was the superior machine; only one feature—the four-wheel drive—lay in favor of the older car, yet this was sufficient. In one of the most exciting races of the series, the Four Wheel Drive veteran sped home a winner, as the Allard, making its final bid to pass, with rear wheels spinning slid off the course on the last turn.

"The success in these road racing and hill climbing activities culminates one phase of our experimental researches," Don Olen, of the Engineering Department, said later.

They demonstrate that the Four Wheel Drive, still without any appreciable modification for hill climbing or road racing, by virtue of its four-wheel-drive principle is superior in power and in safety to the conventional rear drive cars.

Milliken put it more brusquely:

It is something to ponder that there are performance regions in speed, acceleration, and climbing ability which are forever beyond the two wheel drive machine regardless of its design perfection, for there is a limit beyond which it is unsound practically and engineering-wise to try to accommodate more power into two wheels of an automobile. Every one of the wheels by virtue of the weight it supports can sustain a tractive effort. A spinning wheel gathers no acceleration. The logic is self-evident. No four-legged ass ever used only two legs to propel himself.

Long before the Equinox Mountain or Edenvale races, however, the Four Wheel Drive Auto Company had turned for its own safety program to a somewhat less spectacular, but equally rigorous and scientific, testing program, begun in 1930 at Purdue University under the direction of Professor H. M. Jacklin of the Automotive Engineering Division, and had furnished a truck for experimental work, the first of a number of grants to institutions throughout the country interested in research on factors of traction and highway safety. In 1939, in an article appearing in *Automotive Industries,* H. M. Jacklin summarized the results of a series of tests over a nine-year period comparing the performance of rear-drive, front-drive, and four-wheel-drive trucks. The Four Wheel Drive truck had not only proved better on straight, level roads with less danger of slipping the driving wheels and less danger of skidding, but had also been found safer on curves, able "to negotiate sharper curves at the same speed or the same curves at higher speeds than other types of vehicles." The four-wheel-drive principle would therefore permit, well within the margin of safety, the installing of more powerful engines, increasing the acceleration and hill-climbing ability of a motor truck.

In 1933 R. A. Moyer, then at Iowa State College at Ames, later chairman of the Committee on Winter Driving Hazards for the National Safety Council, again with assistance from the Four Wheel Drive Auto Company, had begun his far-reaching research on skid resistance of various road surfaces and, along with Stinson and Roberts of Ohio State, established the yardstick for measuring automotive tractive ability and the skid resistance of various road surfaces in terms of the "coefficient of friction," a ratio of the measured braking force of a vehicle to the weight or load carried in given test conditions, opening a new era in highway construction and vehicular design.

Largely as a result of these investigations Walter A. Olen addressed the annual meeting of the Society of Automotive Engineers in Detroit during the winter of 1934 on "The Effects of Front Wheel Stability on Public Safety," stressing the need for further research on load distribution between front and rear axles in terms of safety and vehicle maneuverability, citing the rotative effect bringing increased weight on the front wheels in case of braking and the wide differential between the weight on the inner and outer wheels of a vehicle on a curve, as well as the varying revolutions of front and rear, right and left wheels in going around a curve, capable of being relieved only through a center differential. Earlier in the same year he had spoken to the Society of Automotive Engineers in Chicago, asking for uniform and intelligent legislation for the operation of motor trucks from coast to coast, both addresses marking him as one of the leaders in approaching highway safety through vehicular design.

By 1934, for instance, traffic accidents had risen to the alarming total of 30,000 people killed annually, with another million injured, and a property damage in excess of $2,000,-000,000. Alarmingly enough, 80 per cent of all accidents were taking place on improved and paved highways and 70 per cent of them at speeds of less than 30 miles per hour. To the problem of highway fatalities, there were then—as now—three general approaches. The one most obvious to the public was that of driver, road, and vehicle regulation. It is necessary to remember that in the early days of the automobile few states, if any, required licensing the driver or imposed any limitations on eligibility to drive a car or truck except the natural ones of ownership or access to the position behind the wheel. A few cities early imposed speed limits on city streets, but on country roads the sky was the limit, or if not, the horsepower of the motor. There were no stop signs, no arterials, no overheads and freeways. Highways were single-lane or double-lane without benefit of center-line marking or the caution of no-passing areas, or signs indicating safe speeds on curves or the rapidity of the descent ahead. There were then, and are today, too few states demanding certification or inspection of the safety mechanisms of the vehicle, brakes, headlights, and tires, and too few drivers' schools. There are even today volumes of complicated regulations from state to state on the length of wheelbase and axle load of commercial vehicles which need to be standardized and made uniform from coast to coast.

And yet public regulation is only one approach to the problem. Of equal importance are the roadbed surface and the climatic conditions affecting vehicular control, since a consistent number of highway accidents and fatalities year after year are due to skidding. A National Safety Council study found that of all accidents involving skidding, fewer than 1 per cent occurred on dry pavements, 18 per cent occurred on wet pavements, and 40 per cent on pavements covered with snow and ice. Here the early researches of R. A. Moyer at Iowa State clearly demonstrated the nature of the problem. The skid resistance of a moving vehicle depends, for instance, directly upon a high value in road and tire friction and upon the speed of the vehicle. The higher the speed, the greater the need for high friction values. Braking tests on dry pavement indicated that the minimum distance required to stop a passenger car on a level road at a speed of 20 miles per hour is between 16 to 20 feet. At 60 miles per hour the distance is increased nine times, or will be between 150 to 180 feet. At 80 miles per hour the minimum distance will have increased sixteen times over that of 20 miles per hour and will demand a range of 260 to 320 feet.

Braking tests on wet pavements gave friction values frequently less than one-fourth or one-half as high as those on dry pavements, which really meant that stopping distances on wet pavements rose as high as 600 to 700 feet at 60 miles per hour, or as high as 1,000 to 1,200 feet at 80 miles per hour, a stopping distance far beyond normal expectations and frequently beyond the driver's ability, no matter how skillful, to steer a straight course on a wet or slippery surface. Most dangerous of all on a wet pavement were the curves where the friction required for braking is superimposed upon the friction required to hold the vehicle on the road or in the allotted traffic lane. On a slippery pavement dangerous side skids were almost certain to develop if, in braking, the wheels were locked on curves or downgrades. Other tests indicated that the stopping distances on wet or packed snow were five times those on dry pavements, and those on wet ice were the greatest of all, demanding approximately ten times the stopping distance the same vehicle would require on dry pavement.

An interesting aspect of later researches carried on by Professor Moyer at the Institute of Transportation and Traffic Engineering at the University of California at Berkeley, still using an FWD, is that friction values of the roadbed or pavement surfaces themselves vary widely. Some hard-surfaced pavements under unfavorable conditions have friction values as low as those of a wet pavement or of ice and snow. Affecting friction values are the age of the pavement, including the amount of oxidation, or weathering, the amount of traffic film accumulated from oil drippings, grease, rubber, and mud; the type and amount of asphalt used on the asphalt pavement and the amount of bleeding involved; the surface texture of the roadbed, whether glazed or polished, coarse-grained or fine-grained, and the rounded and worn or gritty and angular nature of the aggregate or gravel; the construction of the road and the amount of free water left on a roadbed after a rain and acting as a lubricant between tire and road surface. On the basis of the research it has become obvious that it is possible to build road surfaces that provide skid-resistant values for wet conditions nearly as effective as those obtaining on a dry road. As Professor Moyer has written,

> Slippery roads exist because of improper construction and inadequate maintenance, and any road can be made skid-resistant and kept in that condition. Thus it seems fair to state that a "Slippery Road" sign is a confession of faulty construction and upkeep. It is to be regretted that many highway departments still depend on "Slippery Road" signs to warn drivers of a danger which is entirely unnecessary.

The third approach to the problem of highway accidents, again less obvious to the public, is through engineering and vehicular design. From the very beginning Walter A. Olen had been concerned with manufacturing not only a powerful, effective truck, combining speed and economy, but also a safe truck, combining maneuverability with effective traction and braking power. Twenty years before four-wheel brakes had become generally accepted on passenger cars, the Four Wheel Drive truck had already made use of them. In 1945, announcing a gift to the University of Wisconsin of $50,000 to be used in further research on the safety of performance and range of operation of the motor truck, he stated the position of his own company.

> While much progress has been made in the development of the four-wheel-drive principle during the life of our company, much remains to be done. The fact is we have just recently arrived at a truer conception of the marvelous results that can be accomplished by further refinement in our engineering. In our construction of a truck based

on the applications of scientific principles we shall be able to give to car and motor truck transportation everywhere greater safety, and that combined with greater economy and greater speed.

After acceptance of the grant by the University Board of Regents, a Truck Research Project Committee, whose members were Professors Lloyd F. Rader, P. H. Hyland, and K. F. Wendt, was appointed by Dean M. O. Withey of the College of Engineering, and the project placed under the direction of A. H. Easton, an engineering graduate of the University of Michigan with a number of years of experience in the Automotive Division of the Aberdeen Proving Grounds. The broad objectives of the project outlined were to accumulate fundamental data for the design of trucks and highways, with particular reference to four-wheel-drive and rear-driven trucks, the work itself divided into studies of safety, economy, tire wear, the effect of vehicles on pavement, steering characteristics, brake timing, riding characteristics, and engineering performance, including drawbar pull, acceleration, braking, cooling, and tractive resistance. Additional grants of $54,000 from the Four Wheel Drive Auto Company and $10,000 from other Wisconsin industries have helped to carry the work forward.

Among the results of the study, the most insistent one has been the increased tractive ability and the greater safety of the four-wheel- or multiple-drive truck over the conventional rear-drive truck, an advantage ranging from 40 to 80 per cent on slippery surfaces. Overpowering the drive wheels or spinning them, a common enough factor in truck operation, is most apt to result in skidding, or *fishtailing*, and loss of control. Fishtailing occurs when the power is applied to rear wheels only but not when it is applied to the front wheels or all wheels. Operating on a slippery surface, the rear-drive unit is limited in its recovery from the tendency to skid or jackknife, while with the front or all-wheel drive the recovery angle is nearly three times greater and the tendency to go into a skid or jackknife remains at a minimum.

Coupled with factors of greater safety were other equally interesting results. Contrary to popular opinion, the four-wheel- or multiple-drive truck was found to be more economical both in fuel consumption and in tire wear. Application of power to the front wheels caused no measurable change in the steering-effort requirements, and power delivered through the steering wheels minimized the loss of steering control by preventing the locking of the front wheels during a braking operation. The *fanning* technique of brake application, far more effective than the locked wheel in reducing the braking distance in all drives, has also been found to work much better on the front-wheel- or multiple-drive truck than on the rear-drive.

Another area of testing in which the Four Wheel Drive Auto Company played an extremely important and commendable role was in the work of the Committee on Winter Driving Hazards, set up by the National Safety Council and the United States Public Roads Administration to make a thorough investigation of the dangers peculiar to winter driving. Preliminary traction and skidding tests were conducted as early as 1939 on Lake Calhoun near Minneapolis; in 1940 a more comprehensive series of tests was concluded on Lake Cadillac at Cadillac, Michigan. After the Second World War the testing was once more resumed on Houghton

Lake, near Roscommon, Michigan, in 1946; and in 1947 at the invitation of the Four Wheel Drive Auto Company, prompted by Walter A. Olen's intense interest in safety, the winter driving tests were moved to Pine Lake, near Clintonville.

Largely as a result of these tests, recommendations were made that have drastically reduced the hazards of winter driving. Since the braking distance for cars and trucks on glare ice is ten times the distance on dry pavement, and on packed snow is three to five times that on dry pavement, it was recommended that road and city pavements be kept free of ice and snow at all times by prompt removal of snow and by the use of abrasives. The use of chains and operating at reduced speeds were also strongly advised. It was also clearly demonstrated that the old idea that heavier vehicles held to the road better and were therefore capable of greater speeds without danger was erroneous.

By 1950 the results had become clear and conclusive. What the tests had indicated is the greater safety factor in a four-wheel drive whether in the light-duty truck or in the heavier six by six. A six-by-six multiple-drive truck can safely negotiate a curve at speeds up to 15 per cent faster than can a rear-driven truck. It is possible to stop on curves in shorter distances because of the greater control of the front wheels in multiple-drive trucks, the multiple-drive requiring 9 per cent less distance than rear-driven trucks even when both are equipped with four-wheel brakes. What is true of the trucks alone is equally true of tractor-trailer combinations. Brakes on the trailer and rear tractor wheels frequently result in jackknifing. Brakes on the rear tractor wheels alone also result in jackknifing. By far the most stable unit is one in which braking power is applied to all wheels in a multiple-drive unit, where the front and rear traction of the tractor aids in the stability.

In the 1950 tests a careful camera recording of the behavior of trucks on glare ice reveals that in a rear-driven truck, when the rear wheels lock, the truck invariably goes into a spin. In a front-wheel drive, when the front wheels lock, the truck leaves the curve at a tangent. In a four-wheel drive with all wheels locked, the truck continues in the same direction. On the straightaway a similar pattern occurs. On a front-wheel drive there is a tendency to skid sideways. On a rear-wheel drive spinning is inevitable. On a four-wheel-drive truck, the vehicle continues in the same direction.

What has become evident is that the winter-driving hazards in the states of the snow belt can be drastically reduced by the application of motor power to all wheels of a vehicle. What has been clearly proved, too, is the practicability of approaching the problem of accident and traffic safety through vehicular design.

Long before these later tests the Second World War had intervened. By 1950, however, traffic accidents having risen to the disastrous total of more than a third of a million people killed in the decade between 1940 and 1950, with an additional ten million injured, and the accidents having involved a property loss of more than twenty billion dollars, Mr. Olen's conviction about the greater safety of a four-wheel-drive truck had been proved. An eloquent testimony to the original soundness of the principle is that more than half of all the companies engaged in the manufacturing of motor trucks are today producing some type of four-wheel drive.

A War on Wheels

The role of the motor truck in the Second World War has not yet been fully told. In the First World War the transport of men and supplies by motor-driven vehicles had been an innovation, startling and ingenious, sometimes born of desperation and often, in spite of the difficulties of terrain and the inadequacies of highways, amazingly effective. By the time of the Second World War the Army had been fully mechanized, and transportation by motor truck was commonplace both in the Army and in civilian life. The motor truck, however, is not a battlefield weapon. There, the armored-tank, motorized artillery, the tractor, and caterpillar have superseded it. Other weapons, more effective in battle and more spectacular, have eclipsed it: airplanes, the LST landing ships, the amphibious ducks and alligators. Public imagination has been caught by the use of bazookas, rockets, and flame throwers, by the proximity fuse, the guided missile, and radar, by the accuracy of pinpoint bombing, the global range of the B-36, and the destructiveness of the atomic bomb. Interestingly enough, however, in spite of the lack of glamour, the lowly motor truck played perhaps the most basic role of all.

Marc Harris wrote in 1946:

> Probably the greatest unsung military supply wagon of the war was the army truck. More than once, trucks formed the life line of supplies, both in Russia and in France, when railways and other means of transport were out of commission. To the extent that the war was won by superiority of men and supplies on the front lines at a given time, the decisive battles of the war were won by army trucks.

"The greatest advantage in equipment the United States has enjoyed on the ground in the fighting so far," George C. Marshall, General of the Army and Chief of Staff, stated in his biennial report to the United States Secretary of War in 1945, "has been our multiple drive motor equipment, especially the jeep and the two-and-one-half ton trucks."

During the First World War up to November 11, 1918, the American Expeditionary Force had in service 62,891 motor vehicles, including motorcycles. In the Second World War, up to April 30, 1945, there were 710,650 motor vehicles operating in the European Theater of Operations, most of them trucks. In addition, during the years 1943 to 1945 the United States had supplied another half-million trucks to the European Allies on the lend-lease program: 76,736 jeeps and 98,207 trucks to England, and 28,356 jeeps and 218,888 trucks to Russia alone. Equally striking are the figures for motor-truck movement of military supplies, which were always in some stage of delivery and shipment, embarkation, unloading, and distribution. In the First World War between the dates of June 1, 1917, and November 15, 1918, 8,346,342 tons of supplies had been shipped to the armies in France. During the Second World War the total had risen to 47,-641,882 tons. The amount of matériel per man in 1945 was six times that of 1918. In 1918 one round per gun in the artillery had required approximately 102 tons of explosives; in 1945 the requirement had risen to 436 tons. In 1914 in thirty-six hours, beginning September 6, twelve thousand Paris taxicabs had moved 4,985 troops to the first battle of the Marne, a distance of 28 miles. In 1944, between December 18 and January 6, at the height of the German counter-thrust near Bastogne, 220 two-and-a-half-ton trucks and 162 semitrailers of the Motor Transport Service moved 67,-236 troops and 10,800 tons of supplies an average of 100 miles.

The Second World War was almost literally a war of supply. The transportation and communication lines of the United States Army reached more than 56,000 miles, a network encircling the entire earth. It was also the most rapidly moving war of all times and the most ponderous in sheer weight of the matériel required for fighting. According to Lt. Col. Randolph Leigh's summary of the activities in the European Theater of Operations,

> Never before had armies struck by land and air with such sustained speed. Never before had the striking power and velocity of combat forces been so completely regulated by the ability of supply forces to cope with unprecedented burdens. There were no tables of experience for what had to be done. The masters of logistics from past wars would have deemed the task impossible. Finally the fight was won because the men who braved the fire were supported by other men who dared to move mountains.

In the D-day invasion of Normandy, thousands of motor-driven vehicles hit the beach with the first assault troops. In the first 110 days, 500,000 vehicles were driven off the ships and landing barges, up over the beaches, in over the piers, outward from the beachheads and port cities, at the astounding rate of one every two seconds both night and day. Nearly a third of the men landed in the first assaults were soldiers of the Services of Supply, engineers, men of the Ordnance Department, of the Quartermaster, Signal, and Transportation Corps, men of the Medical Corps and Military Police, nearly all of them dependent for the swift and skillful accomplishment of their assigned tasks upon the jeep and the motor truck. Theirs were tasks of hardship and daring, frequently requiring them to range ahead of the combat forces and always to accompany and follow them. They were heavy tasks, many times prosaic and always miserable. Men and motor trucks, covered with grease and grime, lumbered up over the beachheads, moved forward in mud and rain, hauled piles of ammunition to and from dumps in lonely forests, moved endless supplies in and out of bleak warehouses along narrow, muddy roads and across the countryside, built new camps and staging areas. Ammunition dumps turned into churning mire under the grind of wheels, truck transmissions were ground out by the steady low-gear work, brake drums destroyed by seepage of mud and grit, tires torn and cut into shreds by shell fragments, broken metal, and pieces of barbed wire. Men and trucks rebuilt miles of road destroyed by shell and demolition explosives, threw bridges across rivers, strung wires for the Signal Corps, and built camps and staging areas, depots, hospitals, and airfields.

Within two months the bridgeheads of Normandy had burst outward into a vast siege camp, extending across France to the western borders of Germany. In the words of Leigh,

> A completely mechanized overseas force without proper port facilities, without an adequate highway system, and without suitable railway service had chased the most highly mechanized armies that Europe had ever known from their strong coastal positions to their main fortifications, 350 to 700 miles inland.

So rapid had been the advance that at the end of the third month the American Armies held positions which, according to the plans of the campaign, were not to have been theirs until six months later. The task of supply for the rapidly moving Armies was unparalleled in history. Between August 25 and November 16 the Motor Transport Brigade, organized as the Red Ball Express, hauled 410,000 tons of supplies, the route stretching from St.-Lô to Chartres and thence following the advance, until the circuit extended more than 700 miles and became the longest one-way traffic artery in the world. On the peak day the tonnage reached 12,342. To maintain the road, the Army Engineers used five general-service regiments, or 6,000 men. From Cherbourg and the beaches to Dol, between October 14 and 31 the Green Diamond Express delivered 15,590 tons. The Lions Express, operating between Bayeux and Brussels, from September 16 to October 12 carried 17,556 tons of oil, coal, and ammunition. From October 6 to December 13 the White Ball Express carried 140,486 tons from Le Havre and Rouen to Paris. The ABC Express from Antwerp to the northern front began operating on November 30; a month later, by December 31, it had moved 15,536 tons exclusive of petroleum and oil products.

In the European Theater alone Army Engineers repaired and maintained a military network of highways reaching 7,476 miles. After the heavy rains and the winter frosts and thaws of 1944, they rebuilt 2,100 miles of road, rebuilt 223 major highway bridges, and repaired hundreds of others. For the crossing of the Rhine they assembled, built, and repaired sixty-two bridges and used up 100,000 tons of bridging material, 5,000,000 board feet of lumber, 215,000 feet of structural steel, 8,000 feet of chain, 315,000 feet of wire rope, and 6,000 pontoon-bridge floats. Throughout France they had built camps and hospitals, depots and airfields, railroads, pipelines, and waterways. They had constructed accommodations for 122,000 prisoners of war, 5,450,321 cubic feet of closed storage space, and 63,788,785 cubic feet of open storage. At the end of the war they had cut 20,000,-000 board feet of lumber in the Alps and Pyrenees, carried it to and from 125 sawmills in France. Members of the Signal Corps had laid 2,500 long-distance underground-cable circuits, totaling 125,000 circuit miles; rehabilitated 3,300 miles of telephone line; built 1,200 miles of pole-line construction using 20,000 miles of copper wire; maintained a mud-spattered jeep messenger service covering nearly all France from Brest and Cherbourg to Strasbourg and Dijon, Marseilles, Nice, and Bordeaux. Men in Ordnance received, stored, classified, and reissued 500,000 tons of supplies, replacements, and spare parts. In one month the loss of motor trucks reached 10,478 trucks. In another, the Ordnance men of the U.S. Third Army repaired and returned to service 9,000 general-purpose vehicles. For the Medical Corps every day 2½-ton trucks carried cargoes of whole blood to the front line and evacuation hospitals.

But all these figures are for the European Theater of Operations alone. Before Operation Overlord had come the invasions of North Africa, of Sicily, and Anzio. After it was to come the invasion from the south of France, Operation Dragoon, bringing 698,158 troops and 2,594,980 tons of supply. Others had already taken place or were to follow. In the Persian Gulf motor trucks and bulldozers had rebuilt harbors and highways for the transportation of supplies to Russia. Airfields and bases had been built in North Africa, in Australia, in the tangled mass of tropical islands in the South Pacific, from the treeless rocks of the Aleutians to far-off Karachi and Calcutta on the east and west coasts of India. The Stilwell Road from Ledo to Burma was being built through the mountains and jungles to the interior of China, opening a land route to Chungking. The Alcan Highway from Edmonton to Fairbanks was to stretch 1,480 miles across the mountain wilderness of Canada and Alaska. And everywhere from the invasions of Guadalcanal and Tulagi to Iwo Jima and Okinawa, the jeep and the motor truck (along with the bulldozer and the carryall and the Tournapull and the supercrane) had helped the armed forces to move forward, always a useful and indispensable item in the "arsenal of democracy."

For the Four Wheel Drive Auto Company of Clintonville the Second World War, like the First, was a challenge to its productive capacity. The single highest tribute ever paid to the basic principle of the four-wheel drive and the soundness of its engineering, as well as its record during the First

World War, is the fact that long before the outbreak of the Second World War the United States Army had adopted the principle of multiple drive. "A marked improvement in cross-country mobility of tactical vehicles," General Marshall wrote in 1941, "has resulted from the development of the all-wheel drive." Shortly before the end of the First World War the United States Army had bought out the basic patents of the Four Wheel Drive Auto Company for the sum of $400,000. The patents had served them in good stead. In the Second World War all army vehicles from the ¼-ton jeep to the 30-ton heavy-duty haulers, bridgebuilders, and semitrailers had made use of four-wheel or multiple-wheel drive.

The first orders after the outbreak of hostilities had again come from Britain. Two days after the British declaration of war, Mr. Wigmore, formerly of Gaston, Williams and Wigmore, now retired and living in California, organized a new company. Within a few weeks an agent for the new firm who had gone to England carrying information and specifications cabled a request for two trucks, an SU and an HH6, for a series of tests. A few weeks later the first order came for twelve trucks, equipped with earth borers, followed by an order for 500 SU's, an order again doubled before the year was out. During the same year the United States Marine Corps ordered its first sixty trucks to be used for troop landings; from the U.S. Engineers came an order for bridgebuilders, followed by an order from Canada for 221 SU's and HR's, and another order for fifty huge log haulers for Great Britain.

Production figures shot upward. For more than twenty years the company had been operating at a production level of less than $2,000,000 a year, except for 1937 and 1938 when the figure had risen to $4,000,000, only to decline again in 1939. In 1940 the figure rose to $6,000,000. Employment shot upward to more than a thousand, and the men began to work around the clock in three shifts.

With the war in Europe and the likelihood of wartime shortages, domestic sales rapidly rose a full 25 per cent. Highway departments, construction contractors, public-utility fields, and oil producers and city fire departments, suddenly more sharply aware of their own needs, ordered heavily. With the American entrance into the war after Pearl Harbor, the company once more tendered its entire output to the service of the country by a wire to the War Department identical with the one sent to Secretary Baker twenty-four years earlier. To ensure adequate spare parts for the trucks already in use, as well as any new units the War Production Board might allocate to the domestic user, the company purchased the Eagle Manufacturing Company of Appleton, Wisconsin, and moved the manufacturing, assembling, and sale of domestic trucks to Appleton, to clear the Clintonville factory itself for the war effort. As the needs demanded, the factory was reorganized for mass production, a new 8½-acre proving ground was built, and $500,000 spent for new machinery.

Between March 25, 1940, and October 28, 1941, the Congress of the United States had authorized the investment of over $63,000,000,000 in national defense. Speaking on January 6, 1942, President Roosevelt replied to the challenge of the Axis powers with the announcement that the United States would supply 60,000 planes, 45,000 tanks, 8,000,000 tons of shipping, and other war tools in comparable numbers. To many a critic of the administration at the time the figures seemed utterly fantastic. To the Axis powers it seemed uncertain whether the President was bluffing or dreaming but equally certain that the production goals he was calling for were completely impossible. In 1942, however, total war production rose 300 per cent over that in 1941; in 1943 it rose 500 per cent. In 1944 war production alone reached a peak equal to the production of our total peacetime economy. The goals set by the President had been met and surpassed.

In the race for national war production the Four Wheel Drive Auto Company kept the pace. By the end of 1941 the production figures had risen nearly 300 per cent to $16,123,072. At the end of 1942 they were up to $24,028,601. In 1943 they climbed to $39,192,489, and two years later, at the end of the war, they reached an annual figure of $48,000,000. Employment figures had doubled and then tripled, and the payroll alone had advanced from $1,500,000 in 1941 to more than $6,000,000 in 1945. In five years 30,000 trucks had left the assembly line at the rate of more than twenty trucks a day. In the total sum of more than a million vehicles delivered to the armed services by the automotive industry, 30,000 trucks does not seem an astounding number, not to a country accustomed to accepting results in ever larger figures. But to the management of the company, to the workers, to the town of Clintonville and the surrounding countryside, and to the thousands of men in the armed services dependent upon the trucks themselves, it, too, was part of the miracle of production that won the war, and the story from the point of view of Clintonville merits retelling.

There was first of all the question of the workers themselves. At the peak of the First World War production, employment had been around 1,600. During the succeeding twenty-four years the average number of workers employed had been less than half that number. If the factory was now to meet the production goals assigned to it, the employment numbers of the First World War would have to be more than doubled, rising to well over 3,000, and that in a community of less than 4,000 people. To meet the need W. A. Olen once more, as in earlier years, called upon the surrounding communities. "Give me the average farm-born American," he said. "He grew up with a hammer and a pair of pliers in his hand. Out of him a man can make the best machinist in the world." Shortly after the call had gone out, the employment office was interviewing prospective employees at the rate of more than 800 a month. To supplement the local workers, men came driving in from the surrounding farms and from neighboring villages and cities, on buses and in station wagons, on motorcycles and in car pools, in more than 700 share-the-ride programs from towns as near as Embarrass or as far away as Antigo, from which twenty-two employees drove a daily round trip of 110 miles to meet their shift.

As the production figures neared their peak, the variety of workers kept increasing. Supplementing the trained machinists constituting the regular ground force of the factory were more than 500 part-time farmers and farm workers, 250 day laborers, more than a hundred carpenters, a dozen barbers and beauticians, clergymen, postal clerks, cooks, restaurant workers and waitresses, florists and morticians, piano tuners, auto salesmen, dance instructors, postmasters, bill collectors, lawyers, and physicians. To weld them into a working force, skillful, cooperative, and efficient, required patience, ingenuity, tact, and a fundamental faith in the inherent good will and the innate capacities of the average American. "There are two tests for men," W. A. Olen said, in setting up within the factory the first Joint Labor and Management Committee under the War Production Board in 1942.

> One comes when business is poor and we operate at a loss. Some employees always feel then that they are on a sinking ship and get out, though there are always others who simply buckle down and help solve the problems. The second test comes in times of great volumes of business—with our production doubled and tripled many times—when some men worry and lose themselves in the hazards of responsibility. Others, however, rise to the occasion. We have still a great unknown quantity of human ability in all departments that justifies us in moving our production goals forward.

On May 3, 1942, a War Production Drive, following in the wake of the National Production Drive launched by President Roosevelt, was held on the newly completed proving grounds, with a goal of stepping up production by an additional 25 per cent. A huge crowd of 5,000 workers and citizens of Clintonville and the surrounding area gathered in a drizzling rain to be addressed by representatives of the Marines, Federal Public Relations Board, and the War Production Board. "Under our democratic form of government men are not directed to do things by force," Mr. Olen addressed the workers in a concluding speech. "We need to become heroes of production. Every man and woman in our employ has an opportunity to use his ability, his genius, and his ambition."

As an outward symbol of their cooperative enterprise and the essential goal of their efforts—the supply of military weapons to the soldiers in the field—the company organized a drive to supply the United States Marines with a gift truck on the anniversary of Pearl Harbor to replace an older FWD which had fallen into the hands of the Japanese in the capture of Wake Island early in 1942. Each worker in the plant donated three hours of his time, the board of directors paid for the materials, and within two weeks after the initiation of the plan the manufactured truck was ready for delivery to Col. F. S. Robillard, Lt. J. Pauze, and Lt. A. Engle, who accepted it for the Marines, along with a scroll inscribed by each one who had contributed to its construction.

The increase of workers, of course, brought its own problems of transportation, housing, and food production. To alleviate the housing shortage in Clintonville, the company secured allocations for one hundred new housing units in the city. To assist the individual builders, the company bought a substantial acreage north of the plant and, subdividing it, resold it to individual workers at cost. For transient workers the company rented the armory, installing cots, mattresses, and blankets for those compelled to stay overnight during the icy winter weather and snowstorms frequent to central Wisconsin. To protect its own manufactured products, the company bought up and dismantled empty barns and dance halls in the surrounding countryside, moved them to the factory, and rebuilt them into warehouses. It supplied areas for victory gardens for all workers, in 1944 the total produce grown upon them being valued at more than $5,000. The local worker had built the company; it was local workers banding together, the machinists, the farmers, the carpenters, trade workers, the erstwhile waiters and automobile salesmen, who carried the war effort. It was the management that welded them together into a creative force. By 1944 more than 500 workers had left the plant to enter the armed services. The newly organized Military Welfare Department of the company, under the direction of Mildred Olen Dedolph, maintained an active interest in them, receiving nearly three thousand letters and replying to each one, remembering the men with gifts and packages at Christmas time. In September of that year a questionnaire had gone out from the factory, asking how many of them wished to return to their former jobs at the end of the war. An overwhelming majority replied in the affirmative.

Equal to the problem of recruiting workers was the problem of the allocation and securing of materials. Allocations of raw materials and priorities were established by the War Production Board in Washington, but estimates and schedules had to be made out in triplicate, revised, and made again, followed by hundreds of letters and wires, and long-distance calls, and hurried trips to Chicago, Milwaukee, Cleveland, New York, and Washington. Even after the allocations had been secured and priorities established, there were still difficulties of procurement with dozens of firms competing for available supplies, each armed with similar allocations and priorities. During the war years thirty-eight to forty subcontractors supplied items, ranging from wooden plugs to complete axles and transmissions, for the Four Wheel Drive trucks. To secure their delivery on schedule, since one single item could stop an entire assembly line, there was a need for half a hundred expediters, ranging the field from one subcontractor to another, all burdened with their own problems, to see that the material arrived on time (though not ahead of time, since that, too, would create difficulties). To all this was added the problem of transportation. Back in 1911 in the early days of the factory, thirty-two trains a day arrived in Clintonville. Branch lines of the Northwestern Railroad led to Gillett, Oconto, and Green Bay. By 1940 the branch lines had been abandoned and torn out, and the number of trains arriving daily was down to four. Trucks now had to substitute for the railroad. During the peak months of production more than 8,000 truck-loads of material were driven into the factory gates each month to be converted into new trucks. To crate the shipment for the first British order alone, more than 2,000,000 board feet of lumber had to be cut and hauled into the factory from the north woods. To assemble the manufactured trucks more rapidly, the company rented the County Highway Department garage at Stevens Point, setting up a second assembly line and hauling the disassembled parts for new trucks overland in trucks already completed.

War contracts were negotiated on a cost-plus basis. That meant keeping an accurate cost accounting on the first trucks and sets of spare parts, known as the preliminary run, comparing these with costs on the next hundreds of trucks and sets of spare parts, known as the test run, and then renegotiating a contract with an estimated cost for the completion of the order. Except for the additional time and manpower involved, however, this caused no great difficulty. "We have had over thirty years of successful experience in dealing with the government," W. A. Olen told the assembled stockholders in 1942, and throughout all these years we have found that by being frank, honest and thorough in the presentation of our assets, costs, and problems there has always been a sympathetic consideration and a disposition to be fair on the part of the officers of the federal government.

To facilitate war production, nearly a half-million dollars' worth of new machinery had to be bought or leased from the Federal government and installed, replacing worn-out and obsolete tools or increasing the efficiency of the factory. There were schedules of manufacturing to be met, materials and supplies to be secured and brought to Clintonville, an adequate flow of parts to be established throughout the factory, a hundred statistical and analytical studies to be made, and always the endless conferences between engineering and production, between production and management, between management and workers, sometimes ending in drawn-out and tedious negotiations and table-pounding speeches; and always the hundreds of men at work in the foundry, at the forges, on the drill presses and lathes, swinging overhead cranes, operating hydraulic presses, pounding, hammering, riveting, crating, and loading. There were War Bond Drives with a hundred trucks and two thousand workers parading through the city streets; drives for the United Service Organizations; housing committees to be set up; Committees on Civilian Defense; Committees on Safety; Committees on Production with awards to outstanding workers, set up under the War Labor Board; public programs to be launched; publications to be issued to the factory workers and distributed among civilian users to support the government's Truck Conservation Program by Preventive Maintenance, set up under the Office of Defense

Transportation. And all this was part of "the miracle of production" but one achieved not by statistics but by the hands of men and women, by their honest efforts, by their devotion to the job and to public duty, by thought and study, by sleepless nights and agonizing concentration on the job ahead.

On December 16, 1943, in an outdoor ceremony the first Army-Navy E was awarded to the company and token pins presented to the employees, for their "great work in the production of war equipment," by Capt. Howard Wright, Lt. Comdr. E. H. Jones, and Colonel Slezak, Deputy Chief, Chicago Ordnance District. "In a tragic hour of necessity, your country had a critical job for American industry to do," said Colonel Slezak, reading the citation.

> Part of that job was placed in your hands . . . and you did not merely a good job . . . something to get by inspectors . . . but a magnificent job. You fulfilled the trust your country placed in you.

A second Army-Navy E was awarded in July, 1944, a third in February, 1945, a fourth in August. The Army Ordnance Banner had been awarded in April, 1944, and a Treasury Bull's Eye Flag for employee war-bond subscription in January, 1944.

At the time of the Army-Navy E award in February, W. A. Olen was confined to the hospital at Rochester, Minnesota. At four o'clock telephone engineers entered his room and plugged in a loud-speaker. Lying there in the hospital bed, he listened to the program praising the efforts of his company, the men and workers who were carrying on. At the conclusion of the speeches, in a ceremony rebroadcast to the workers, two Army officers entered the hospital room and pinned an E on Mr. Olen. Mr. Olen that day wrote, in a letter to the workers,

> Every workman on every machine in the plant, every person who has contributed the material in every branch of the company's activities, have all contributed to this fine record. It is the sum total of about three thousand men and women who have given conscientious and efficient service every hour of every day that has brought this about.

In the meantime thousands of Four Wheel Drive trucks had left the factory and were operating on the battlefields and in far-flung areas. In England as a special service, FWD trucks equipped with the utility field earth borer had already dug out ten thousand delayed-action bombs dropped by German warplanes. Twenty-five per cent, and in the larger cities as high as 50 per cent, of all bombs dropped had been those of delayed action, some of them boring into the earth 10, 20, and 30 feet, waiting there, hidden, for the unexpected moment when the time mechanism would set off a shattering explosion, destroying buildings, killing and maiming the inhabitants or passers-by. Bomb-disposal squads located the hidden metal by an electrical device registering depth; then an FWD roared to the scene no matter what the terrain or amount of street rubble, set the giant earth borer twisting like a corkscrew, removing the earth to a depth where skilled workers could excavate the bomb before explosion. In England alone the Four Wheel Drives had saved thousands of lives and millions of dollars in property damage.

In France and on the Normandy beachheads, in the Red Ball Express, in the Green Diamond and the White Ball, single Four Wheel Drive trucks had hauled three thousand tons of munitions, clothing, gasoline, food, and supplies per week, consuming 25,000 gallons of gasoline, traveling in convoys of fifty trucks at 25 miles per hour through the darkened night without headlights along the narrow roads and between hedgerows. At the end of the campaign hundreds of giant bridgebuilders—six-wheel drives with a 60-ton capacity and a 200-horsepower motor, powerful enough to go anywhere—had helped to throw bridges across the Rhine.

Down on the Persian Gulf at Bandar Shahpur and Khorramshahr other FWD's had helped to rebuild the ports from a 25,000- to a 260,000-ton monthly capacity and, with the ports rebuilt, had repaired, regraded, and built a road along a camel trail 644 miles across the desert to Kazvin, an Iranian village at the foot of the Elburz Mountains, and in the months that followed joined in the truck caravans rolling up over 97,000,000 miles in hauling supplies to Russia through one of the most arid and difficult countries in the world. Far to the east on the way to the Burma Theater, shiploads of trucks, unloaded at Calcutta, had been moved by railway to Ledo and thence were running in convoys over the newly built Stilwell Highway across a thousand miles of jungle and mountain wilderness to Kumming, every twenty-fifth vehicle carrying extra food and every third a load of extra fuel, the convoys accompanied by surgeons, dentists, technicians, and a chaplain.

In the Canadian Northwest more than 300 Four Wheel Drives, purchased by the government from the county and state highway departments, had built the Alcan Highway from Edmonton to Fairbanks across a vaguely mapped virgin wilderness of mountain streams, swamps, bog, and muskeg, one of the greatest road-engineering projects of all times. Late in 1943 a convoy of fourteen trucks, thirteen of them FWD's, had made a 1,354-mile trip, from Edmonton to Camp Canol at Norman Wells, over a route no motor truck had ever traveled before. Carrying 6-ton loads, the trucks had left the military highway at Peace River and, winding northward to Fort Alexander, crossed the western end of Great Slave Lake and Lake Mills on the ice, and then had pushed 500 miles further, over frozen streams and unimproved log bridges, across muskeg barrens to Fort Norman on the Mackenzie (where the natives turned out to see what they had never seen before, a self-propelling motor vehicle) and then plowed the last 39 miles up over Vermillion Heights to Camp Canol.

Celebrating the end of the war on V-J day, W. A. Olen addressed nearly 3,000 workers—men from the factory, secretaries and office workers, file clerks and department heads, engineers and foremen.

> We are grateful that the war is over. It was a war won largely by men and women who work with their hands . . . with the hands like yours who make things . . . with the hands of soldiers who use the things made by hands like yours . . . with the hands of nurses and Red Cross workers and surgeons who bind up the wounds. We are the greatest people on earth to work with our hands. What our hearts desire and our minds will, that we can do with our hands. It is the secret of our success and our national greatness.

It was as fine a tribute as had ever been paid to the American workers and soldiers and to the results achieved by the united effort of heart and hand.

A Second Generation Takes Over

In 1952 the Four Wheel Drive Auto Company had been in operation for forty-two years. During that time the employment figures had varied from thirty men to well over 3,000. Working conditions had changed. The 10- and 11-hour day and the 60-hour week had given way to the 8-hour day and the 40-hour week. The wage rate had periodically risen —and fallen in the thirties—from an average of 25 cents an hour to well over $2 an hour. The unorganized shop had given way to a company union and then itself been superseded by the United Automobile Workers' local. But in all that time not a single day had been lost either to the workers or to the company through a shutdown, a strike, or a lockout—truly a remarkable record.

There are a number of factors responsible for the harmonious relationship existing in the company between management and labor, but certainly one of the most important ones has been the attitude toward the men they employed of the board of directors, influenced and directed by the attitude of Mr. Olen. "The most basic fact in our business," he said as early as 1917, "is that men, and not machines, build our trucks. It is sound business to pay good wages, and to keep every man who starts, working for the company. Every man will then take an interest in the business, because it is every man's business." "The Wisconsin laborer cherishes his freedom," he said, speaking to the Wisconsin Bankers' Association in 1942: "he enjoys voting as his conscience dictates; he holds the right of free speech close to his heart; and he would willingly sacrifice all that he has for his own freedom of action."

They are statements indicative of a fundamental attitude deeply ingrained by his own experience. It is sometimes necessary for, and frequently characteristic of, a business executive to be decisive in his answers, harsh and even brutal in his disregard of the human factor where wages and company profits are concerned. The sentiment of good will toward his own workers becomes then a persuasive technique in handling men or indeed a kind of public sentimentality, covering the basic rigor with which private decisions involving profits and wages are made. The basic question is really one of the presence or absence of a fundamental good will. Henry Ford was both acclaimed and damned for having established the five-dollar day. Was the concern really for the welfare of labor or the adherence to an economic theory that ultimate profits depended upon the ability of the worker to consume? The welfare of the wage earner in Clintonville has been dependent, of course, upon the welfare of the wage earner in all industry, but the good will that exists between management and labor depends less upon economic theory than it does upon the simple factors of sympathy and understanding.

Mr. Olen still recalls the belittling shortcomings of his own youth. As a child he was both tongue-tied and snub-nosed. He still remembers the poignancy of discovering the latter when two Indian lads, playing on the old medicine grounds bordering on the farm, saw him and, hiding behind trees, each alternately put his finger to his nose and pushed upward, pointing toward him and grinning at each other. It took forty years before he met people easily, he says, though he was gregarious by nature and loved to associate and work with others from childhood onward. Even as a youth, he was sensitive and anxious to please rather than envious, and given early to projecting himself imaginatively into the lives and roles of others. For more than seventy years it has kept him from thinking exclusively of his own point of view or his own or the company's problems.

He has also been and remains today an indefatigable reader, having for forty-odd years, in addition to discharging his duties as president and general manager of the company and a host of civic responsibilities, devoured books at the rate of three or four volumes a week. His tastes have always run toward history, varying widely from the early history of the local scene and the lost village of Questationong to ancient Egypt and the far-off Himalaya or Antarctica. From his reading has come a perspective, a sense of time within the timeless, which, coupled with a surprising physical vitality, has brought not only an unusual perspicacity but a pervading optimism wherever the human factor is concerned. "I believe in talking things over," he is fond of saying, because if the problem is stated to enough people, some one will come up with a better solution than any we have tried before.

How big is a man? How much trouble can he handle? Hire people who can do something far better than you can, and then make it easy for them to do it the way you want it done.

Two volumes which played perhaps an inordinate role in his own early thinking, growing up as he did in the midst of the Populist movement in the late nineteenth century, were Edward Bellamy's *Looking Backward* and Ignatius Donnelly's *Caesar's Column*. From the first he acquired a sense of the dignity of labor, ennobling the hard chores of his own childhood. From it he acquired also a strong sense of civic obligation, the responsibility of the individual for the social welfare of the group. From *Caesar's Column*, that rather weird fantasy contemplating the final overthrow of a capitalistic society, once a best seller and now forgotten, the youthful, impressionable mind received an intimation of the holocaust into which mankind could be swept if it were to become locked in a struggle between a moneyed oligarchy and a secret world-wide federation of organized workers. The great fear of the Orwell of the 1880's was anarchy, not regimentation. The death throes of the modern world were not to be uniformity and passivity, but murder and rapine and fire, ending in the midst of the general slaughter and destruction with 250,000 slain capitalists entombed layer upon layer in a monumental circular tower of concrete, rising like a pyramid from Union Square. "I was only fourteen when the book swept the country," Mr. Olen says. "In the sleepless night after I finished reading it, I resolved that if it were ever given me to be an employer of men, I should deal justly, love mercy, and walk humbly before God." Though he learned to take the book less seriously later on, this vision of the ruthless and corrupt tyranny of wealth and the inevitable rise to power of an enslaved and embittered labor, a vision of the modern secret police, the dirigible, world-encircling airlines, and a television of mirrors (though curiously enough Donnelly makes no reference to the horseless carriage or the motor truck), remained with him. "I was ready to accept the inventions," Mr. Olen says, "but I wanted nothing to do with the methods that led to Caesar's Column."

But the motivation was less a fear of labor than a sense of justice, a seeking to understand the worker's point of view. The first trouble in the factory arose as early as 1915. With the company busy on its first substantial order from the British government, employment had doubled, and then tripled to 110 workers, and the company had imported an efficiency engineer from one of the larger motor corporations. He had driven the men ruthlessly, demand following demand. On the morning of September 9 a delegation of workmen called upon Mr. Olen, "respectfully requesting" that the efficiency engineer "be removed from the position he holds." "He makes unfair advances on the working men and causes confusion between us and our employers. If he is not removed all of us will leave the factory." The paper had been signed by 110 men. The deadline had been given as the next morning. Mr. Olen followed his first inclination. He called a meeting of the entire working force, asked them to state their grievances, invited the efficiency engineer to reply. Before the consultation was over, the efficiency engineer had voluntarily resigned, and the men were ready to return to work with a doubled zeal.

The incident set a pattern for future relations, whether the working force numbered 110 or 3,000. At the time of the episode wages had averaged 20 to 25 cents an hour. By 1937 the average hourly rate had risen to 50 and 60 cents. Under the social legislation of the thirties the workers had organized a company union, wages had been increased by nearly 50 per cent, the 40-hour week had been stabilized, the rights of collective bargaining recognized, unemployment compensation, accident, and sickness insurance had been established for the workers. All of this, of course, met with violent criticism in Clintonville, as it did throughout the country. In addressing the company's stockholders at the annual meeting in 1938, Mr. Olen met the issue squarely.

> I know the general feeling is that if a business is not successful, labor ought to share in the loss with the stockholders. But labor says, no. Their attitude is that they have no voice in the management and they are therefore not responsible. There is a market for labor and they feel entitled to the market price. I do not say this is right, but I do say they are within their rights, and I accept their decision.

He had expressed himself similarly elsewhere. "Collective bargaining, the eight-hour day, the forty-hour week, and a minimum wage law," he said, addressing the National Truck Manufacturers' Association, "will tend to drive the chiselers from business or make them adhere to the ethics of fair industrial enterprise."

The reasonableness of the attitude paid off. In the next year, in the midst of the recession of 1938 and 1939, sales had fallen off by nearly a hundred per cent and the company was faced with a serious operating loss. The question of a reduction of wages was presented to the workers. They were given a full and complete account of the current state of the business, including files from the accountant's office. The matter was debated hotly. On the first vote labor was divided; on the second the majority voted against any readjustment of their wages. Then some of the older men spoke up. "I feel it is up to us to take a cut," one of them said. "I have worked here for twenty-two years and I don't think the management is telling us any falsehoods. I am not forgetting that company wages built my house, bought my cars, raised and educated my family. I say, let's take the first step." On the third occasion the union voted unanimously to accept a readjustment of wages to be worked out by the executive board of the union and company representatives, a readjustment that in some cases went as high as 24 per cent.

During the Second World War years the company union was superseded by a United Automobile Workers' local, and the salaried workers established a salaried-employees union. The company recognized the principle of the union shop and established a modern industrial-relations division, concerned with all phases of employment—hiring, firing, wage negotiations, the safety and welfare of the worker, incentive pay, job evaluation, and aptitude testing; promotion and transfer, personnel, recreational, and vacation activities. Through the job-evaluation and aptitude-testing program every employee was channeled into a job where he could move ahead. Grievance committees were established, in recognition of the right to dissent; 1947, a typical year, produced forty-six grievances, thirty-six of them settled by foremen and supervisors, eight of them by the grievance committee, and two by arbitration. Annual vacations on pay were established for the workers.

"We are happy in our industrial relations," Robert Olen, son of W. A. Olen, was quoted as saying in an article in the Milwaukee *Journal* in 1947, shortly after he had become general manager of the company. "We have made genuine progress and we have not bought our labor peace."

"We are well satisfied with the provisions of our new contract," the union president said in 1944, the year most of the changes had taken place. "We have a better contract and superior conditions to those most unions have been able to obtain after many years of negotiation."

In 1952, at the annual Old Timers' Banquet, nearly four hundred men and women sat down at the tables to celebrate their own long-time association with the company and the completion of Mr. W. A. Olen's forty-second year as company president. Many of the other men associated with the founding of the company and its direction in the earlier years had died. Charles Folkman, the department-store owner, who had been one of the first to subscribe for stock in the newly reorganized company in 1910, an early member of the board of directors, and the first vice-president of the company, had died in 1929. Frank Gause, the depot operator for the Chicago and Northwestern Railroad, one of the first men interested in organizing the company and the first secretary of the board, had died in 1941. Otto Zachow, who had lived to see his own invention and the company he had helped to organize affect the destiny of his country and the entire world, and who in later years again became associated with the company, had died in 1942. W. A. Holt and C. W. Priest, both early directors, had died in 1930. Antone Kuckuk, a director of the company since 1914 and later vice-president, had died in 1946. Charles Hagen, the cheesebox manufacturer from Black Creek, one of the first purchasers of a Four Wheel Drive truck, one of the original investors and a director of the board from the beginning, later president of the Eagle Manufacturing Company, a subsidiary at Appleton, had died at the age of eighty-five in 1947. Joseph Cotton, who had kept a faithful record in the pages of the Clintonville *Tribune* of the early exploits of the inventors and the first four-wheel-drive car ever built, later an investor in the company, a member of the board, advertising and sales manager and president of the Four Wheel Drive Auto Company of Kitchener, Ontario, had died in 1949. D. J. Rohrer, owner of the sawmill and lumberyard in Clintonville, one of the original investors, company treasurer, and vice-president after 1947, had died in 1950.

Present for the occasion and still active in the company were men like Harry B. Dodge and B. G. Donley, company engineers; S. H. Sanford, treasurer, and D. M. Russell, comptroller; Herman Koehler, who had begun operating a lathe in the first machine shop back in 1910; Frank Dorn, driver on the first Army test run from Washington, D.C., to Fort Benjamin Harrison in 1912; Chauncey Williams, later factory superintendent, and Ward Winchester, who had driven FWD's for the Pershing expedition into Mexico; Joe Leyrer, expert machinist and toolmaker, who will tell you, "It's because of men like me that they call this the old people's home"; Jim Sorenson, world-famous metallurgist, who loves to recall P. J. F. Batenburg's crisp "The faster it goes, the better how is it"; and Floyd Hurley, who became assistant factory superintendent in 1916, later director of manufacturing, and who says laughingly, "We have fun around here. Most of the men I know personally—hell, I hired most of them." Others had retired but were still interested in the company. Many had seen their own sons grow up and join the company, as engineers, or in the production, the advertising, and the sales departments.

In 1952 the Four Wheel Drive Auto Company had passed the $500,000,000 mark in commercial sales. It had paid out over $65,000,000 in wages to the workers of Clintonville and the surrounding community, having given employment during its history to more than 20,000 men and women. During the same period the capitalization had increased from $110,-000 to $6,000,000. Twenty-five million dollars had been paid out in local, state, and Federal taxes. In the meantime Clintonville had grown from a village of 1,800 to a town of nearly 5,000. Fortunately it has never lost its essential characteristics as a small rural town. Other towns have become submerged in their industrial development, the leisure of the streets transformed by the hurried pace of industry, the factory chimneys outtopping the church spires, railroad switching yards and warehouses encroaching upon residential areas, flimsy and shabby factory houses crowding the sandy, treeless lots around the manufacturing plants. Clintonville, on the other hand, has grown slowly and steadily.

Much of this owes itself to the wisdom of the company management and local government working together. The factory has never depended solely upon the citizenry of Clintonville but has drawn from, and contributed to, the surrounding farmlands and smaller communities. During normal years the company has followed a policy of scheduling its production to dovetail with agriculture. In the fall and winter, with crops harvested and the slack period at hand, truck manufacturing reaches its peak. In the late spring and summer, in the season of planting and harvest, the factory operates with a reduced staff. More than half of the workers are farm owners, and more than three-quarters live on farms or in neighboring towns and villages.

During the thirties, with hundreds of families on relief rolls in the larger towns of Waupaca County and with many a farmer in the community in danger of losing the title to his land, Mr. Olen made a systematic check of the relief rolls of cities like Waupaca and New London, as well as the records of delinquent taxes on farms, inviting both groups to part-time employment in the factory to help offset their financial difficulties. "There are 10,000,000 unemployed workers in the United States today," he said on one occasion,

> who are like the lost tribe of the Fox Indians. The real solution to their plight is not charity but a chance to work. . . . The government cannot legislate prosperity but industry can create it. It is up to us, to industry, to create jobs for them and to help them find useful occupations.

But if Clintonville grew slowly in size and population, it has grown steadily—particularly in those things which make for comfortable and amiable small-town living. The clay and mire of the unpaved streets in 1907, which provoked the original inventors to concern themselves with a four-wheel-drive principle, have long since, here as elsewhere in America, been replaced with concrete and asphalt. The country road leading into town has become U.S. Highway

45, linking Clintonville to the cities of the Middle West, to Milwaukee and Chicago, and opening a thoroughfare for thousands of folk, from Illinois and Iowa, Indiana, Kansas, and Missouri, to the surrounding lakes and recreation areas of Wisconsin and northern Michigan. In 1918, at the close of the First World War, Joe Cotton had listed the needs of the town: new school buildings, a city hall, a new hotel, an auditorium, a new railroad station, an enlarged public library, a park, and a hospital. The following year the new high-school building, at that time "one of the finest in the state," was completed at a cost of $200,000, the first in a continuing program of public-school needs still being carried forward. In the same year the Four Wheel Drive Auto Company made a special appropriation to be used for securing additional volumes for the Finney Public Library, erected the year before with the aid of Carnegie funds. In 1921, the city, aided by state funds and a special appropriation on the part of the businessmen, erected an armory building at a cost of $31,800, providing both for athletic activities and a meeting place in lieu of a needed city auditorium. In 1927, a group of businessmen and the officials of the company joined in forming a corporation for the erection of the new, modern Marson Hotel, still one of the best in the central part of the state. In 1931, after a long series of acquisitions of various parcels of land and donations by various individuals, including D. J. Rohrer and W. A. Olen, a 28-acre tract lying on both sides of the Pigeon River and adjacent to the business district was turned into Central Park by the cooperative effort of hundreds of workers, manufacturers, and businessmen who donated their time to reclaim and improve the swamp and slough area along the river. In

1950, a new municipal hospital for the city and surrounding territory was completed at a cost of more than $800,000, financed by a gift from the company of $65,000 and individual contributions solicited under the direction of W. A. Olen, general chairman for the fund-raising committee.

The new railroad station which Joe Cotton had called for did not materialize, primarily because of that change in the transportation world which the very trucks his own company was building had helped to bring about. To replace it, however, several businessmen of the city and various officials of the Four Wheel Drive Auto Company organized the Clintonville Transfer Line, which in 25,000,000 miles of hauling has carried away the city's products and brought back to it the needed products and produce of the rest of America. A similar group of company officials and businessmen have organized the North Central Airlines and, with the aid of a gift from the company, built one of the finest small-town airports in the state, carrying mail, express, and passengers throughout a territory reaching from Detroit and Chicago to the twin cities of St. Paul and Minneapolis and as far west as Fargo, North Dakota, bringing to Clintonville itself hundreds of factory visitors, sales representatives, domestic users, and foreign importers from every area of the globe.

In all of this the Four Wheel Drive Auto Company has played a central part both directly and indirectly. Throughout the years since its first organization, the company has contributed over a quarter of the annual city taxes. During the last fifteen years it has contributed a third of a million dollars in outright gifts to the community hospital fund, to a memorial for veterans, to the city athletic fund; to the Red

Cross, the Boy Scouts, and the American Legion; to the community airport; to the support of educational institutions in the state, the University of Wisconsin and Lawrence and Ripon Colleges. In 1948 it created the Four Wheel Drive Foundation for benevolent purposes, with an annual appropriation from the company of $20,000 to $30,000. More immediate and direct than any gifts, however, has been the participation of the company's employees, the factory and salaried worker, as well as the management and the board of directors, in civic affairs. "Our stockholders, employees, and directors are a part of the community environment," Mr. Olen is fond of saying. "Our employees are at their place of business for an 8-hour day, but they are a part of the community for the full 24." In the city council, on the school board, on the board of directors for the library, on the park and athletic commissions, company men are leaders in civic groups and activities. Mr. Olen writes:

> The Four Wheel Drive Auto Company believes that a corporation is a corporate body of individuals, collectively and individually charged with all the duties and responsibilities of citizenship. We do not believe that a democracy can exist or survive with organizations in its midst, whether individually owned or corporate, whose sole purpose is to make money for the stockholders, and whose sole responsibility is to remain within the law, without any regard for that larger area where men working together and for each other advance human rights and contribute to human progress.

On July 10, 1952, exactly forty-two years after he had become president of the Four Wheel Drive Auto Company, W. A. Olen asked to be relieved of his duties as president.

For many years he had been the oldest executive in the truck-manufacturing industry. Expressing his gratitude to the board of directors and to other members of the company for the many years of friendly association, he suggested that his successor be chosen as soon as possible, so that the employees, the stockholders, the suppliers, the dealers and banks, as well as the public, might know "who my successor is to be in order that the uncertainty of old age will be removed."

Two months earlier, on May 8, Mr. Olen had been honored by the University of Wisconsin in its Engineers' Day awards. Recognizing him as the oldest truck manufacturer in the United States in years of service, the citation praised him for his eminent professional services, as "a manufacturing executive, who through foresight and administrative ability founded and developed an important Wisconsin industry, promoted safety through highway research, and who has shown unselfish devotion to public welfare."

Acting on Mr. Olen's request to name his successor, the board of directors elected his older son, Robert A. Olen, to succeed his father, Walter A. Olen retiring to the chairmanship of the board. Robert had been general manager of the company since 1944, a member of the board of directors since 1947, and had become vice-president in 1949. He had been with the company for over twenty years, having begun his work in the machine shop, where he had become a foreman in the derrick department, later a member of the sales department, and then successively held positions in the advertising department and served as secretary to the president. Don Olen, the second son, had become a manufacturing executive of the company, served as director of the engineering division, and had become works manager. A number of other young men had come into managerial positions. James Driessen had succeeded D. J. Rohrer as treasurer of the company and become a member of the board in 1950, and acted also as assistant general manager. G. F. DeCoursin had become general sales manager; H. P. Sell had become treasurer, acting as an assistant to S. H. Sanford; G. D. Simonds was heading the engineering division. Old faces had given way to new ones—a second generation was taking over.

But the problems of the Four Wheel Drive Auto Company are by no means over. They are different problems now from those which had faced Otto Zachow, Walter A. Olen, Frank Gause, D. J. Rohrer, and the other members of the company and the board of directors, but they are no less real. The Second World War has again been followed by a period of readjustment and by a temporary slump in the truck market and by new engineering demands for field operation and truck service. The motor truck has become an increasingly specialized vehicle, calling for new refinements in engineering, for an extended program of research, testing, and experimentation. The earlier 3-ton Model B has been superseded by an entire series of models ranging from the LD, with a gross vehicle weight of 11,500 pounds, to the giant ZU six by six, with a gross vehicle weight of 60,000 pounds, with ever-new possibilities in range and power, in flexibility and adaptability, emerging on the engineering horizon. Manufacturing and management have become extended into a vast system of specialized departments: industrial relations, with its emphasis upon aptitude testing, grievance committees, cost-of-living adjustments, training programs, benefit associations, credit unions, and safety programs; production scheduling, to allay the evils of seasonal and periodic employment; buying research; purchasing; subcontracting; plant engineering and maintenance; stockkeeping; standards and productivity; cost estimating; engineering; parts and service (with a volume of $3,500,000 a year); sales; advertising; public relations; financing: each of them now a very highly specialized service calling for infinite detail.

Nearly half of the stock in the company is still held by the small investor, the majority of the stockholders still live within the state, and a good portion of it is still owned by Clintonville residents.

"We are proud of our record during the forty-two years of our existence," Robert Olen said in addressing the stockholders in 1952.

> Out of a total investment of $906,000 we have produced earnings of $9,500,000 or over ten times the investment, paid cash dividends to our stockholders of over $3,700,000, paid stock dividends of $2,250,000, and present a financially sound company with a net worth of $6,727,000 currently doing a business of over $30,000,000 a year.
>
> We shall continue our efforts to develop an increasingly stable and profitable market, to provide steady employment at fair wages for our employees, to fulfill our obligations to our community, to our state, and to our nation, and in so doing we are going forward in the faith that as we contribute a real service to the transportation world, we shall ourselves continue to grow and prosper.

But whatever the future is to hold, one cannot gainsay the past achievement. The first half of the twentieth century has been variously characterized. Certainly the most singular phenomenon has been the transformation of the physical scene and the living habits of the American people: in communications, in travel, in mechanization and machinery, in housing and dietary habits, in the conquest of disease, and in longevity. On the whole, it has been an era of abundance, though also at moments one of acute want. It has been an era of two world wars and an intensive and prolonged business depression, for which the capitalistic structure of our economy has received its full share of blame. It has been an era of social change and of extensive social legislation that has brought to the worker a recognition of his full status in our economy and granted him the right to share in the profits and benefits, as well as, to some degree, to assume his own obligations. It has been an era of private and corporate enterprise, more recently and in an increasingly nostalgic vein referred to as *free*.

But in its most basic sense no enterprise has ever been *free*. In an era when private and corporate enterprise was less subject to state and Federal regulation, it was still subject—and more so than now—to the fluctuations of our general economy, to competition, to supply and demand, to the limitations of human ingenuity, engineering, and managerial skills, and wherever operating at its best to a sense of responsibility for the public welfare. It has not been the freedom of American enterprise but its voluntary assumption of the limitations and, in a larger sense, of the obligations under which it operates that has distinguished capitalistic enterprise at its best; not freedom alone, but responsibility in freedom that constitutes the best in the American way of life. And it is exactly this recognition of the human factor, whether in the strength of men working together, in the rights of labor to its hire, or in its concern for the public welfare—the utility and safety of its product—that has distinguished the history of the Four Wheel Drive Auto Company under the direction of Walter A. Olen. "If a thing works," he has said,

> if it does the job it is meant to do—if it strengthens the human arm in providing the bounties of life, and in doing so, endangers none—it is beautiful. Our best service is to create wealth in a greater measure than we consume.

Notes and Acknowledgments

CHAPTER ONE

For the early history of Clintonville the files of the *Tribune* have been indispensable. For the courtesy of being allowed to disrupt the busy routine of a newspaper office with innumerable requests for materials and assistance, my thanks to Ward Risvold and Carl Turner, then editors, and to Mrs. Viola McIntyre of the *Tribune-Gazette* staff. The statement from Edison is quoted in *The Horseless Age,* vol. I, No. 2, as having originally been made in an article appearing in the New York *World,* November 17, 1895. For the story of Otto Zachow and the experience leading to the idea of a four-wheel drive, I am indebted to his son, Clarence A. Zachow, president of the Atlas Conveyer Company, Clintonville, Wisconsin. All materials relating to the organization of the Badger Four Wheel Drive Company and, later, to the Four Wheel Drive Auto Company are, unless otherwise indicated, taken from the recorded minutes of the meetings of the board of directors, from the annual statements to the stockholders of the company, or from private correspondence.

CHAPTER TWO

For the story of the contribution of Otto Zachow and the ball-and-socket four-wheel-drive principle to the development of the jeep, see Christy Borth, *Masters of Mass Production,* The Bobbs-Merrill Company, Inc., Indianapolis, 1945, pp. 209-214. For many of the details on the history of the Olen family and the early life of Walter A. Olen, I am indebted to Nora and Valberg Olen, sisters of Walter A. Olen, residents of Winneconne, Wisconsin. The meeting of the Clintonville Advancement Association on April 10, the July 14 Booster Day celebration, and the description of the State Fair at Milwaukee are from the pages of the *Tribune.*

CHAPTER THREE

The story and results of the Washington–Fort Benjamin Harrison test run in 1912 were widely reported and commented upon at the time. See *Power Wagon,* March 1; *Commercial Car Journal,* April 15; *Automobile Topics,* April 20; and *Commercial Vehicle* for May. In 1946, A. E. Williams, former brigadier general, then retired, retold the story in *U. S. Army Automotive Transport History,* published by the Four Wheel Drive Auto Company. Other details are taken from newspaper accounts along the route as indicated.

CHAPTER FOUR

An article on the Dubuque–Sparta test by Lt. J. W. Bollenbeck appeared in *Outdoor World and Recreation,* March, 1913. An earlier article by David Hartshorn had appeared in *Power Wagon,* September, 1912. Other details are taken from the *Wisconsin State Journal,* Madison, Wisconsin, and from reports of the drivers, Frank Dorn and Chauncey Williams.

CHAPTER FIVE

The best account of the motor truck in the Mexican campaign is an article by Rollin W. Hutchinson, "The Army and the Motor Truck," originally appearing in *Review of Reviews,* October, 1916, later reprinted by the Four Wheel Drive Auto Company.

For the role of the motor truck in the First World War, I am indebted to James R. Newman, *The Tools of War*, Doubleday & Company, Inc., New York, 1943; Ludwig Renn, *Warfare*, Faber & Faber, Ltd., London, 1939; Wilde, Popper, and Clark, *Handbook of War*, Houghton Mifflin Company, Boston, 1939; T. H. Wintringham, *The Story of Weapon and Tactics from Troy to Stalingrad*, Houghton Mifflin Company, Boston, 1943; O. L. Spaulding, *The U. S. Army in War and Peace*, G. P. Putnam's Sons, New York, 1937. The quotation from Sgt. W. J. Rickenbacker is from a letter to the company, dated February 11, 1919. The letter from F. L. Crowhurst was an unsolicited communication to Walter A. Olen and company officials.

CHAPTER SIX

A useful study on the history of early road building is the volume assembled by Clyde King, *The Automobile: Its Province and Its Problems*, in the *Annals of the American Academy of Political and Social Science*, vol. CXVI, November, 1924. The quotation on the trip across the plains is taken from an article in the volume by William Joseph Showalter. A second useful volume has been Charles L. Dearing, *American Highway Policy*, Brookings Institution, Washington, D.C., 1942. The experiences on a Western trip are from Winfred Hawkridge Dixon, *Westward Hoboes*, Charles Scribner's Sons, New York, 1921, an entertaining volume now out of print. For much of the story of the role of the motor truck in highway building and maintenance, particularly the role of the FWD, I am grateful to Walter Root and Charles Kinderman of the Iowa State Highway Department, to Fred Putney of Lincoln, Nebraska, to Dick Carlson of Denver, and to Russell Stalnaker of Sacramento, California.

CHAPTER SEVEN

The story of the development of the motor truck is told in A. E. Denham, *Twenty Years' Progress in Commercial Motor*

Vehicles, 1921-1942, prepared for and published by the Automotive Council for War Production, Detroit, 1942. Useful also has been *A Chronicle of the Automotive Industry in America,* prepared by the Automobile Manufacturers' Association, Detroit, 1949. A more general study is Lloyd Morris, *Not So Long Ago,* Random House, Inc., New York, 1949.

CHAPTER EIGHT

All figures on the increase of electric power, as well as those for the telephone, are taken from the *Statistical Abstract of the United States Census,* prepared by the U.S. Department of Commerce, for the periods indicated. The story of electric power has nowhere been written so dramatically across the American landscape as in California. I am grateful to the members of the public relations staff of the Pacific Gas and Electric Company and particularly to Roy Bordeau of the Southern California Edison Company for much of the information regarding the role of the motor truck in the development and maintenance of the electrical industries. Much of the material on the fire trucks is from the pages of the Clintonville *Tribune* and from issues of *The Drive News,* a company publication. An interesting article on the daily life of a New York City fireman, featuring one of the FWD aerial-ladder trucks, appeared in *The Saturday Evening Post,* August 21, 1948. For the material on the Halliburton Oil Well Cementing Company I am indebted to a number of the officials and workmen in the company, particularly to C. P. Parsons, vice-president, to W. R. McClendon, general superintendent, and to George E. Jenkins, superintendent of transportation.

CHAPTER NINE

Two interesting studies on the growth of the motor-truck industry have been made by the Automobile Manufacturers' Association: Franklin M. Reck, *Horses to Horsepower,* 1948, and *Motor Truck Facts* in various annual editions. More inclusive studies of transportation are S. L. Miller, *Inland Transportation,*

McGraw-Hill Book Company, Inc., New York, 1933, and Ford K. Edwards, *Principle of Motor Transportation*, McGraw-Hill, 1933.

CHAPTER TEN

An early test of the relative hill-climbing ability, safety, speed, and traction of a four-wheel-powered vehicle as against a rear- or front-drive had been made by two German engineers, H. Kluge and H. Kohl, and reported in *Fahrgrenzen der Kraftwagen*. The research sponsored by the Forschungsgemeinschaft Trilok, Karlsruhe, had found a superior performance on the part of the four-wheel drive in all factors listed. Part of the early tests at Purdue under the direction of H. M. Jacklin had also been concerned with the efficiency of the transmission of power from the engine to the driving wheels, where a value of 88.2 per cent had been found for the FWD, an exceptionally high figure for a motor truck. For much of the technical material in this chapter I am grateful for the kind assistance of William F. Milliken, Jr., of the Cornell Aeronautical Laboratory, of Ralph A. Moyer, now research engineer, Institute of Transportation and Traffic Engineering, University of California, and of A. H. Easton of the University of Wisconsin. Much of the work of Mr. Moyer and the results of the work directed by him as chairman of the Committee on Winter Driving Hazards has appeared in the publications of the National Safety Council. Two studies on the skid-resistance properties of road surfaces are "Skid Resistance Measurements," Western Association of State Highway Officials Reprint No. 10, and "Road Surface Properties," Highway Research Board Bulletin No. 27. Mr. Easton's work has appeared in "Traction and Stability of Front-, Rear-, and Four-wheel-drive Trucks," University of Wisconsin Engineering Station Reprint No. 197, and in "Two and Four Wheel Drives Compete in Brake and Traction Tests," reprinted from the *Commercial Car Journal* for December, 1950.

CHAPTER ELEVEN

The quotation from Marc Harris is taken from *The United States in the Second World War*, Barnes & Noble, Inc., New York, 1946. The quotations from General Marshall are from *Biennial Reports of the Chief of Staff of the United States Army to the Secretary of War, July 1, 1943, to June 30, 1945*. The quotation from Leigh, as well as many of the figures on the motor truck in the Second World War, are from *American Enterprise in Europe* (C.M.P. Historical Section, ETOUSA), June, 1945.

CHAPTER TWELVE

A brief discussion of the relation of the Four Wheel Drive Auto Company to the growth and development of the city of Clintonville appears in R. J. Colbert, "Community Progress Created by Small Plants," Community Development Service, vol. 3, No. 3, Bulletin of the University of Wisconsin, University Extension Division, Madison, 1950.

INDEX

National Safety Council, study involving skidding, 157–159
Nebraska State Highway Department, 93
Neopit, Wisconsin, fire, 117–118
New London, Wisconsin, 48
fire, 117
New York Auto Show, 146
New York City, 118–120
New York Motor Club, 5
North Carolina State Highway Department, 93
North Central Airlines, 196
Northern Indiana Law School, 19

Oldfield, Barney, 148, 150
Olen, Clarence, 17
Olen, Don G., 153–154, 198–199
Olen, Otto, 17, 18, 20
Olen, Robert, 191, 200
president of company, 198
Olen, Walter A., addresses, Advancement Association, 23
Automotive Engineers, 155–156
Wisconsin Bankers' Association, 185
director of company, 25
early years, 16–21, 186–188
Fourth of July address, 1905, 3
general manager of company, 29
Miller, Cora, wife of, 20
president of company, 26
retires to chairmanship of board, 197–198
suit against, 80–81
University of Wisconsin, Engineers' Day Award, 198
Olen and Olen, attorneys, 2, 3, 20

Pacific Gas and Electric Company, 114
Packard motor truck, 65, 92

Parker, J. A., 42
Peerless Automobile Company, 61, 64
Pennsylvania State Highway Department, 106
Pennsylvania Turnpike, 106
Pierce-Arrow motor truck, 92
Pikes Peak Ocean to Ocean Highway, 89
Pinkerton Detective Agency, 51
Postal Telegraph Company, 113
Premier Motor Corporation, 73
Prenzlow, Julius, 25
Priest, C. W., 192
Purdue University, 154–155
Putney, Fred, 94

Rambler car, 13
Red Ball Express, 168, 181–182
Reo car, 5, 7, 8, 11, 13, 14, 27
Rickenbacker, Sgt. W. J., 75
Ripon College, 197
Rohrer, D. J., 2, 22, 25, 26, 85, 192, 195, 199
Roosevelt, Franklin Delano, 172–173
Root, Walter, 94
Rose, Mauri, 149, 150
Rural electrification, growth of, 113
Russel, D. M., 192

Sampson motor truck, 36, 49
Sanford, S. H., 192, 199
Schauders' Shoe Store, 2
Selden patents, 57, 58
Sell, H. P., 199
Simonds, G. D., 199
Society of Automotive Engineers, 156
annual meeting, 1934, 155
Sorenson, James, 100–101, 192–193
Sports Car Club of America, 151
Spowart borer, 135

214